What readers are s(
How to W
HEARTFELT LETTER!

C000230634

"A 'must have' for every household and business! I love this book. It takes the guessing out of how to express yourself. Lynette Smith has created an easy step-by-step reference filled with valuable suggestions to help you write heartfelt letters, regardless of the situation, that will be cherished forever."

—Sharon Lund, DD, Author, *Sacred Living, Sacred Dying: A Guide to Embracing Life and Death*

"In a world where so many people think talking to and communicating with each other just means sending a text, what a breath of fresh air to see *How to Write Heartfelt Letters to Treasure*. When you use this book to write your own letters, you and those in your life will be touched in a most wonderful way."

—Robert Wolff, Author, *If I Only Knew Then What I Know Now: The Lessons of Life and What They're Trying to Teach You*

"Your attitude in life makes all the difference in the world and determines how life occurs for you. The most powerful attitude you can choose is gratitude. In this book, Lynette has provided a unique set of tools to facilitate your ability to both express appreciation and adopt gratitude as an everyday attitude. All you need is to add pen, paper, and your heart."

—Scott Hunter, CSP, Business Coach, Certified Professional Speaker, Author, *Unshackled Leadership*

"If you appreciate sending uplifting letters to family and friends, this book begs to be on your reference shelf. Lynette Smith gives you various ingenuous ways to share those tender and heartwarming messages."

—Eleanore Rankin

"The world has changed in many ways, but the need to express gratitude and sincere feelings has not. *How to Write Heartfelt Letters to Treasure: For Special Occasions and Occasions Made Special* is the perfect guide for acknowledging and celebrating the many events that friends, loved ones, and colleagues experience in a lifetime. While not discouraging email and instant communication, Lynette Smith provides the rationale, offers extensive tips on approaching sometimes-touchy situations, and suggests tools and even appropriate times to present personal and business communications. You will cherish this book as a companion to which you can return again and again."

—Flora Morris Brown, Ph.D., Author, *Color Your Life Happy*

"Letter writing seems like a lost art in the age of technology, having been replaced by emails, cell phones, and texting. *Heartfelt Letters to Treasure* has resurrected this meaningful form of communication for all ages and situations. From personal appreciations to business thank-you's and everything in between, Lynette Smith offers tools and tips on planning, packaging, and presenting special letters that will touch the heart of the recipient."

—Andrea Glass, Ghostwriter, *WritersWay.com*

How to Write
HEARTFELT
LETTERS
TO TREASURE

*For Special Occasions and
Occasions Made Special*

LYNETTE M. SMITH

How to Write
HEARTFELT LETTERS TO TREASURE
For Special Occasions and
Occasions Made Special

LYNETTE M. SMITH

DISCLAIMER

This book is designed to provide helpful information on writing heartfelt letters to treasure and is sold with the understanding that the publisher and author are not engaged in rendering legal, accounting, medical, or other professional services. If such expert assistance is required, the services of a competent professional should be sought. Readers are solely responsible for their own choices, actions, and results, and are therefore admonished to exercise good judgment when composing and presenting these letters or other expressions of appreciation. The author and All My Best shall be neither liable nor responsible to any person or entity with respect to any loss or damage caused, or alleged to have been caused, directly or indirectly, by the information contained herein.

Published by All My Best
5852 Oak Meadow Drive, Yorba Linda, CA 92886
www.GoodWaysToWrite.com

ISBN (Print):   978-0-9858008-0-2
ISBN (ePub):   978-0-9858008-1-9
ISBN (Mobi):   978-0-9858008-2-6
Library of Congress Control Number: 2012911108
First Edition 2012

To Byron and Rachael
for Their Inspiring
Gifts of Love

CONTENTS

PART 3
WRITING FOR OCCASIONS MADE SPECIAL

PREFACE

Seems like everyone these days believes writing letters is a lost art. True, letter writing for the most part has given way to occasional jotted notes in a greeting card or email-style letter sent to a fellow computer user. Then, of course, mass-produced annual letters mailed to friends and relatives each holiday season still exist, although in fewer numbers all the time.

But a real letter? The kind that's thoughtfully written—by hand or on a computer—with only one recipient in mind? A rarity.

What have we lost as a society, as individuals, by allowing this not-so-fleeting form of highly personal communication to drift away?

Bonding. That's what we've lost. And a sense of giving appreciation and being appreciated. As a result, we've sacrificed the forming, strengthening, and even rebuilding of meaningful relationships.

This personal story illustrates how heartfelt letters can create enduring bonds of appreciation.

On November 21, 2008, my husband and I attended the wedding rehearsal dinner of our son, Byron, and his fiancée, Rachael. That evening, they surprised us when the two of them each made a special presentation to their respective parents—a beautifully framed, one-page heartfelt letter. Their best man and maid of honor read the letters aloud as Byron and Rachael each stood beside their own parents.

Each letter described what they had treasured about growing up in their family, what they had especially appreciated about each parent, and what values they had learned and planned to bring to their marriage.

We were deeply moved—all of us: four parents, bride and groom, and the rest of the guests. And I can tell you, those framed letters will always hold a place of honor in our homes. To this day, whenever I tell someone about that night and our treasured letters, my hand automatically moves to my heart. That's where I still feel the experience. And my love and appreciation for our son who expressed *his* love and appreciation for my husband and me so beautifully has truly strengthened the bonds we already felt.

And then there's the flip side. Most news stories tend to be upsetting or even frightening. I believe steady exposure to this kind of negative input can cause us to feel depressed, demoralized, frightened, helpless, or even angry. Is that good? Of course not.

I am convinced we can restore the joy, the hopefulness, the generous spirit we could be known for by writing letters of appreciation. Such letters reward both the writer and recipient. Thoughtfully considering all the ways to appreciate someone else—and putting those thoughts into a letter—can strengthen the bonds even before the letter is presented. For both, a heartfelt letter of appreciation can even be life changing.

Have you noticed? In this fast-moving world, people rarely take time to express their appreciation for another. Consequently, many have no idea what a difference they've made in someone else's life. But if they were told—in a letter meant to be read again and again—not only would they feel grateful, but they'd be inspired to do even more good in the world. Every time they'd read the letter, they'd feel just as good as the first time. That's definitely how my husband and I feel whenever we reread Byron's letter!

Can you see, then, how writing such simple expressions of appreciation in letter form might turn our world around, one relationship at a time?

Look at your own relationships. Who are you grateful to have in your life? Would you like them to know, in a very special way, how important they are to you? The tools provided in this book help you express your innermost thoughts in ways that will warm their hearts—and yours. Let's get started now!

LYNETTE M. SMITH

FOREWORD

You are holding an extraordinary book.

Lynette Smith has amassed a wealth of information that will help readers of all ages and backgrounds as they ponder how—even why—to write letters to their friends, relatives, work associates, and others. Who better to write this book than Lynette? She is a pro—a copyeditor, a businesswoman, and an avid letter-writer herself.

I'm excited about being involved in this project because Lynette espouses exactly what we promote at The Emily Post Institute: positive relationships. In this fast-paced world with its complex demands, 24/7 media, and technological advancement, how people interact with each other is more crucial than ever. Whether verbally or through written means, treating each other with respect and consideration is increasingly important.

The foundation of *How to Write Heartfelt Letters to Treasure* is based on two key human traits. The first is crystallized when considering this quote from a favorite book of Lynette's, *The Four Agreements* by don Miguel Ruiz: "The word is pure magic—the most powerful gift we have as humans...." What we say (and how we say it) is the basis for all interactions with one another. The second human trait is that relationships are paramount. Lynette stresses that the words written in letters have the capacity to "grow, enhance, or even rebuild personal and professional relationships."

There you have it: Words bring people together. They have the ability to make—or break—relationships. These facts lead to the reality that thoughtfully written letters can weave strong bonds among people. And this book shows you how to craft those letters for all occasions—letters you'll want to write and send.

How to Write Heartfelt Letters to Treasure is a definite motivator. Lynette's tips will inspire you to write that letter you've been putting off. I know firsthand; reading this book inspired me! It gave me the incentive to write and send a condolence note to a friend who had recently lost her husband. I'd been procrastinating (after all, some letters just aren't easy to start), but writing that letter made me feel good. My friend tells me my note made her feel good, too.

Lynette has a knack for encouraging her reader to be confident and write from the heart. I hope you will gain the confidence and incentive to do the same—to sit down and write heartfelt letters to people you care about.

Lynette is an artist who sees the beauty within. She is also an excellent teacher and a talented coach and mentor. When reading this book, you'll absorb her enthusiasm. She understands that today's letters may be either on paper or via the computer. It's no surprise she favors the beauty and long-lasting quality of a paper version, but she is realistic about emails being a vital way to communicate, too.

The best advice? Just get to it: Write those letters! Lynette does not judge; she encourages. She does not intimidate; she motivates. She simply makes letter writing easy and enjoyable—and I'm sure she will inspire you to want to write more once you get started!

How to Write Heartfelt Letters to Treasure offers simple instructions. In Part 1, The Basics of Writing a Treasured Letter, Lynette reminds you to relax and be authentic while encouraging you to "let your thoughts flow on paper as if you were speaking" and "think about the person you're writing to." She provides a content-sequence formula for composing letters and an Appendix filled with myriad words you might want to use to describe someone special. It also provides sample opening phrases, inspirational quotes, and more.

Whatever the purpose of your correspondence, *How to Write Heartfelt Letters to Treasure* offers you options, advice, and encouragement to write. I'm confident you'll agree this book is a fabulous guide that will jumpstart your letter-writing skills and enjoyment. Your bonus will be enhanced relationships—a plus for you and for every person who receives one of your heartfelt letters.

PEGGY POST

DIRECTOR OF THE EMILY POST INSTITUTE
AND CO-AUTHOR OF
Emily Post's Etiquette,
18TH EDITION

AUGUST 2012

How to Use This Book

When using this book, you can go directly to the advice you need, then write the type of treasured letter you want. Simply skip the types that don't apply.

To get familiar with all this book offers, though, take these five suggested steps first.

1. Skim the chapters in Part 1, The Basics of Writing a Treasured Letter, and jot down notes that apply to your letter and the person you're writing to. Feel free to refer often to this section as you develop your letter.

2. Thumb through Appendix A, Heartfelt Words to Describe Someone Special. Pick the list (more than one may fit) that best applies to the person you're writing to and jot down a few words from the list(s) that appeal most. For example, if the person you're writing to is a young man entering a religious order, check Lists A5 (A Younger Man) and A11 (Someone Religious or Spiritual). Or if you're writing to your newly promoted employee, your primary (or perhaps sole) source will be List A13 (A Supervisor or Employee). But you could also choose supplemental words from the appropriate age- and gender-specific lists (A5, A6, A7, A8, A9, or A10).

3. If you'd like to include an inspirational quotation within your letter, visit Appendix B, Inspirational Thoughts to Quote in Your Letters, and read whichever condensed list of themed quotations

best applies to your letter's content. For example, if you're writing a letter to your daughter and son-in-law to celebrate their first-time parenthood, you would go to Appendix B, Section B3, Children, Parents, and Grandparents, where you might select the following quotation to begin your letter:

> *When you put faith, hope, and love together,*
> *you can raise positive kids*
> *in a negative world.*
>
> —Zig Ziglar

4. If you're writing your letter for a special occasion, go to Part 2, Writing for Special Occasions. Read the appropriate chapter and section for advice on writing about the occasion you have in mind. Or, if your letter is intended for a type of commemoration, search Part 3, Writing for Occasions Made Special. Find the chapter and section that best apply. In either case, jot down ideas you can incorporate into your unique letter of appreciation. Trouble getting started? Visit Appendix C for dozens of phrases to jumpstart your sentences.

5. Write as much as you can first, and then refine what you write. For your first draft, your priority is expressing your thoughts of appreciation, not perfecting the letter's organization. In your next draft, sequence the contents into whatever makes sense to you and fine-tune what you've written. Read what you've come up with, making sure the spelling, grammar, and punctuation are correct and that your letter flows well. Get help in these areas if needed.

Follow these five steps and you'll create a heartfelt letter of appreciation that will be highly treasured by the person who receives it.

PART 1

THE BASICS OF WRITING
A TREASURED LETTER

PLAN IT

Think about the person you're writing to. Would your recipient prefer a longer letter or a shorter one? If you think your letter might be displayed, keep it to one page and consider framing it nicely. Otherwise, handwrite or print the letter on only one side of the paper and present it in one of the ways suggested in the Package It chapter.

Honor your recipient by writing a letter on paper rather than an email letter. Not only does a carefully written, hard-copy letter make a better impression, but it's easier and more reliable to store long term. Your email letter could easily be lost in a computer crash, buried in volumes of other emails, or forgotten altogether.

Of course, you'll write what a wonderful person your recipient is. As you gather your thoughts, focus on appreciating the admirable things he or she has done, as well as the wonderful person your recipient is. Mute the negatives. Avoid saying what could have been done better or how he or she could have been a better person.

Use attractive stationery. Especially if your letter is likely to be framed, choose high-quality stationery in a neutral color that looks good in a frame. Otherwise, you could choose elegant pastel stationery that matches your recipient's favorite color or harmonizes with the color scheme of the event honoring your recipient. Find out the colors being used for a wedding or special birthday party.

If you're planning to frame your letter, first buy your frame and optional mat board. That way, you'll know how much writing space is available. You can give your recipient display options by purchasing a frame that can be hung on the wall or placed on a shelf.

When writing a multi-page letter, number the pages at the bottom. Because you won't be stapling or clipping your pages together, including page numbers will make the sequence clear.

Protect your letters from water damage or humidity. If you hand-write your letter, use permanent ink. If you compose your letter on a computer, use a laser printer for printing if you can, as inkjet printing runs. Otherwise, print your letter on standard white paper and then pay for a quality photocopy on the stationery of your choice.

Make your letter neat and easy to read. If you handwrite it, place a boldly lined piece of paper beneath your stationery as a tracer to keep your writing straight. If you compose it on a computer, select an attractive, easy-to-read font and point size.

Dress up your handwriting with color and texture. Use colored or black ink that looks good on your stationery. You can vary the thickness of your writing with a felt-tip or fountain pen.

Stay away from the edges of the paper or frame. Allow at least ¼" (0.25") of white space between your writing and the inside edge of the frame or mat board. If your letter won't be framed, allow at least ½" (0.5") margins on all edges. If you plan to bind the pages of your letter, decide the type of binding you'll use early on. Then make the bound-edge margin wide enough for the writing to be easy to read near the binding.

If your letter is to be written jointly (for example, from parents writing to their adult child), decide who will handwrite it. If you both write legibly, consider taking turns writing each paragraph. Otherwise, the parent who has neater handwriting can write the entire letter—except for the other parent's signature, of course.

WRITE IT

This chapter discusses writing your letter in general terms. Use the valuable tips you find here to start, and then add more information based on the tips in Part 2 or 3 relating to your specific occasion.

Give yourself quality time in a quiet environment to get in touch with your feelings. Before you set pen to paper or fingers to keys, take slow, deep breaths to quiet your mind and tune in to your heart. Then start writing.

Express your unique writing style. Let your thoughts flow on paper as if you were speaking. That way, your letter will convey that it came from you and *only* you. Will your letter be formal, informal, humorous, poetic, or a combination? Select whatever writing style feels natural to you and will appeal to your recipient.

Apply this content-sequence formula when writing your special-occasion letter:

1. *Start with a salutation.* Write "Dear" and then follow with whatever you normally call your recipient(s), for example, "Mom and Dad," "Bill," or "Sis." Follow the last word with a comma and capitalize the first letter of each major word within your salutation.

2. *Describe a treasured memory* and/or a brief overview of your experiences together.

3. *Describe qualities you admire and have appreciated about the recipient.* This section can be one or more

paragraphs. To help you decide which qualities to focus on, refer to the one or two most appropriate lists in Appendix A and jot down the words from these lists that best describe the person you're writing to. If your letter is directed to more than one person, dedicate a paragraph to each individual, starting that paragraph with the person's name followed by ellipses (...) or a dash (—) or a comma (,).

4. *Describe the positive impact your recipient has had on you.* Explain how this person has touched, changed, or improved your life or career.

5. *End your letter with a complimentary close.* Choose what seems most natural: "Love," "With love," "Affectionately," "In gratitude," "Your devoted (son/daughter)," or "With appreciation." Note that only the first word of the complimentary close is capitalized.

6. *Handwrite your name on the line below the complimentary close.* Use only your first name in a more personal letter; for a more formal, career or business related letter, leave three blank lines after the complimentary close, type your full name, and then above it sign either your full name or your first name. (Learn more about how to set up a business-oriented letter in the Part 3 chapter, Thanking a Product Creator or Stellar Service Provider.)

Let your writing flow logically. A one-page letter to your parents might contain an introductory paragraph, another about one parent, another about the other parent, and then a closing paragraph. If you're writing to your true love, a one-page letter might contain an introductory paragraph, another about your past together, another about your love's qualities you admire, another relating to your hopes for the future, and then a brief closing paragraph. You can elaborate on any of these in a letter that's longer than one page.

Choose a theme, if you wish. Theme ideas: Journey, Growth, Enrichment. You could even choose a comical theme. For example, if you're writing to your parents, it might be "How did you ever survive my childhood?" Or if you're writing to your true love, a comical theme might be "Could any two people be more different?" You can even turn to song titles and build on them in your letter. Think serious ("Stand by Me") or humorous ("Mission Impossible"). Alternatively, pick a casual theme and compose your letter to read like an informal conversation. Most important, choose a theme that's meaningful to your recipient and also resonates with you. As they say, "It's all good."

Keep your letter positive, loving, and truthful. In your approach to writing, be genuine in your praise and write what you mean from your own perspective. For example, because it reflects your personal opinion, "I appreciated your cooking" is better than "The food you cooked was always perfect."

Think about the roles your recipients have played in your life. Write about specific roles that contributed to your development as an individual. Some parental roles might include family provider or kitchen chef; coach, teacher, or tutor; cheerleader, friend, or confidant; disciplinarian, mediator, or nurturer; problem solver, volunteer, or hero. Roles for your true love might include entertainer, organizer, handyman, mechanic, chef, problem solver, guru, inspiration, supporter, cheerleader, empathizer, friend, confidant, hero/heroine, or protector. You get the idea.

Choose words that describe your recipient. Appendix A, Heartfelt Words to Describe Someone Special, contains 15 lists. The first 10 describe a small child, pre-teen child, teen boy, teen girl, younger man, younger woman, middle-aged man, middle-aged woman, older man, and older woman; the last 5 describe someone religious or spiritual; a military service member; a supervisor or employee; a teacher, coach, mentor, or student; and a product creator or stellar service provider. Your letter can cite examples that describe the qualities you chose. Alternatively, you can point out which traits have helped you form your own values and character.

This fun idea can apply to someone of any age: Focus on one word that best describes your recipient. List the letters of that word down the left; next to each of those letters, write a small paragraph or statement that begins with the respective letter of that word, as poet Amber Montoya has done:

Mother's Day Poem

M – is for the memories we have shared
O – is for the outstanding person I see in you
T – is for all the things you have taught me
H – is for the kind heart you have
E – is for everything you have given and shown me
R – is for the remembrance I will have of you

Copyright 2000, 2012 by Amber Montgomery Montoya;
reprinted with permission

Add other creative touches to your letter, if you like. For example, you could insert a relevant quotation at the top of the letter or after your signature. In slightly smaller type, you'd use italics and center this quotation horizontally. If the author is known, write the author's name in the same size type (but not italics) on the right-hand side or center of the next line, preceded by a long dash (—). See Appendix B, Inspirational Thoughts to Quote in Your Letters, for a convenient selection of quotations in these 10 categories: Age; Appreciation; Children, Parents, and Grandparents; Forgiveness; Legacy; Love and Friendship; Spiritual Faith and Devotion; Military and Patriotism; Leadership and Teamwork; and Teaching, Learning, and Striving. (To find more quotation sources, visit Resources at GoodWaysToWrite.com.)

In a long letter, you could insert a brief poem after your signature. Make sure the poem you select is in the public domain and not copyrighted, or write one of your own. Use italics and indent the lines slightly on the left and right, with the title centered at the top of the poem and the author's name on the next line. If you're the poet, state your own name. (To find more poetry sources, visit Resources at GoodWaysToWrite.com.)

Write down your thoughts of appreciation as the main goal of your first draft. In your second draft, you can rearrange the contents in whatever way makes sense to you and then fine-tune what you've written. But first, draft your heartfelt thoughts as if you were talking to the person.

Rewrite it until your letter reflects your best effort. Are you satisfied with how it reads? Does it say what you want it to say? Good. Now have someone else review your letter for errors. Even if you're good at spelling, punctuation, and grammar, you may be too close to your own work to spot every problem. Get help from a friend or professional whose language skills you admire. Then review the corrected revision to make sure it still reflects your own writing style. (Refer to *Free Writing Tips from All My Best* at the Writing Tips tab of AllMyBest.com.)

PACKAGE IT

Make your letter neat, attractive, and easy to treasure. After all, you've put a lot of effort into writing it. If you're presenting letters to multiple recipients at the same time (for example, to both sets of parents when you marry), use the same type of packaging for each letter. Uniform treatment conveys equal status. Actually, it's fine to have subtle color variations in stationery, ribbon, folder or binder, or wrapping paper if you wish.

Frames. The frame holding your letter can be considered its own package (assuming your letter is only one page). Keep your frame free of dust or smudges; store it out of sight in a protected place until you're ready to present it. Alternatively, once you've made sure your framed letter is clean in all respects, wrap it carefully in the most attractive special-occasion paper you can find. Then hide the gift until it's time to present it.

Display jackets. Some display jackets resemble a hardcover book on the outside. When you open the display jacket, you see each page of your letter (up to four pages) nicely mounted on the inside. If your letter is fewer than four pages, consider displaying a poem and/or an inspirational quotation on the inside cover.

Pocket folders. Multi-page letters can be packaged in other ways, too. One idea is to place the pages flat within a pocket folder, tying the color into your theme or established color scheme. On the front, mount a special photo and then place an attractive label below it with your name and the date.

On the inside, place all pages of your letter in the right-hand pocket.

Scrolls. You can roll the pages together like a scroll. Make the scroll big enough that, when opened, the pages will lie somewhat flat. Tie the scroll with a satin or lace ribbon that harmonizes with your theme or color scheme. Into the bow of the ribbon you can tie an attractive tag bearing the name of your recipient.

Other binding. Visit your local copy center to see if it offers an appealing cover and binding that will look special (please, *not* coil binding!) yet will hold up over time. Remember to leave a wider margin on the side you will be binding.

Caution. If your letter is laser printed and will be folded in thirds and placed in a standard, business-sized envelope, fold it with printed side outward. This will prevent "ghosting" on the front of the letter. That happens as toner from the printed surface adheres to the adjacent surface when the envelope and its contents are subjected to high temperatures from mail processing and sorting equipment.

Visit Resources at GoodWaysToWrite.com for more framing, packaging, binding, and gift-wrapping sources.

PRESENT IT

Once you've written and packaged your letter, think about the best way to present it. Let the occasion and the intimacy of the letter direct you.

If you're writing multiple letters, use the same presentation method for every letter. A uniform treatment conveys equal status and enriches the experience for everyone involved.

Consider the following presentation ideas that range from very private to very public.

SPECIAL OCCASIONS

Special birthday celebration. If it would please your recipient to have guests hear the letter read aloud, then do that. But if your recipient might be easily embarrassed or the content of your letter is too personal, then present it privately.

School- or military-related graduation. If you're celebrating the graduation with a party, that's the perfect time to present your letter. Read it aloud if you think your grad wouldn't feel embarrassed; otherwise, simply present your letter on the day of graduation just before or after the ceremony.

Romantic occasion. If you're writing an intimate Valentine's Day letter to your true love, present it while you're having a quiet dinner or drink together. Candles add ambiance, but make sure there's enough light to read by. If your letter is meant to publicly declare your love at a special anniversary party, then by all means read it aloud to your lover. Encourage the guests to pause and honor the moment with you.

If you're celebrating your love privately, then pack a lunch, paper, pens, and a picnic blanket or two, and visit a secluded natural setting, perhaps near a running stream. The quiet time spent there provides a wonderful opportunity to write love letters to each other.

For a romantic "un-occasion," cook your true love's favorite dinner, set a romantic table with cloth table linens, candles, and fine china, and then serve your culinary delight while wearing a "delightful" outfit you've specially selected. Next to your lover's place setting, leave a sealed envelope bearing his or her name. It contains your handwritten letter professing your love and perhaps even describing your special plans for "dessert" together.

Wedding. If you're the bride and groom presenting one-page framed letters to each other, you could formally read them during your rehearsal dinner, sharing the contents only with your closest friends and relatives. Or, to reveal more about the two of you to your wedding guests, you could make a highly public presentation at your wedding reception. But do this only if both of you feel comfortable adding this to your other wedding-day responsibilities. Concerned about losing your composure while reading the letter? Then designate your best man and maid of honor as readers. That way, while the letters are being read, you and your loved one can hold hands and take in the meaning of the words.

If you're presenting letters of appreciation to your respective parents at this time, surprise them at the rehearsal dinner with the special gift you have created. This gesture becomes especially memorable if they had no previous hint of your intentions. Assuming you can keep your composure, read your letters aloud yourselves; otherwise, ask your maid of honor and best man to read them as you stand nearby. If the letters are more than a page, then read brief excerpts.

You can consider doing this presentation at the wedding reception, but only if you're confident all parties would feel comfortable about it. Inviting your parents to stand beside you as the letters are read would be a nice touch.

If you're the parents of a son or daughter getting married, ideally you'll have collaborated with the other set of parents about writing a letter to their own son or daughter, too. (Remember, having a unified ceremony conveys equal status among the families.) If the letters' contents are highly personal, present them before or after the rehearsal dinner. Otherwise, having a public presentation at the rehearsal dinner can be openly enjoyed by all. Again, if you don't want to read the letters yourselves, designate a reader from the wedding party.

Once presented, consider displaying the framed letters in the foyer before the wedding ceremony begins. That way, guests can enjoy reading them before they're seated. Having them on display can set a special tone for the special day.

However, if the letters are deemed too personal and private for everyone's eyes and ears, present them privately or, if the geographic distance is too great, send them in the mail.

Mother's Day, Father's Day, Grandparents Day. Strive to present your letter personally on the official holiday, perhaps with flowers or after a celebratory meal. If the honoree lives far away and you cannot be there personally, then mail your letter. Be sure to mail it "flat" to prevent bending or exposure to moisture during transit. Place your letter with a piece of cardboard behind it into a protective plastic sleeve, then seal the plastic with tape. Also tape the sides so the letter and cardboard stay together. Gift-wrap this flat, sealed container and then place it in a flat 9" x 12" or 10" x 13" regular or cardboard mailing envelope addressed to your recipient.

Cultural or religious rite of passage. If a party, banquet, or intimate celebratory meal is associated with the occasion, that's the perfect time to present your letter. If the letter's contents are appropriate for a public reading, read it aloud when you present it. If not, gift-wrap your letter and hand it to the honoree, either at the celebration or in private.

Career-related occasion. If you're celebrating an occasion such as retirement with a party, it would be fun to present your letter there, especially if it's a signed group effort. But if the letter's contents are meant to be shared only with the recipient, then a private presentation or mailing is appropriate.

OCCASIONS MADE SPECIAL

See the section in Part 3 for presenting your special letter for these people or during these situations:

- ◆ Between a non-retired teacher and a current or former student
- ◆ To a mentor or coach (not a school coach)
- ◆ Between a school coach and one of his or her athletes
- ◆ To a special friend
- ◆ To an aging loved one
- ◆ To a friend or loved one in hospice care
- ◆ To a special individual from someone in hospice care
- ◆ To attendees at a memorial or funeral service (as a formal eulogy or brief oral tribute)
- ◆ To a deceased relative or friend (as a meaningful personal ceremony or tribute)
- ◆ To someone with whom you wish to mend a torn relationship

ENHANCE IT

Let the occasion itself spark your imagination. What would be fun and highly appropriate? What would generate a fond memory?

One idea is to make a video of yourself reading your letter. The video can complement the written letter you'll present or take its place. But do this only if you can speak and read expressively. Be sure to look into the camera lens frequently as you read. Rehearse until you're comfortable speaking and being filmed. Ask the videographer to use a tripod, select a plain background, and arrange proper lighting in a noise-free setting. Wear clothing that's neutral—nothing that will distract viewers from your face and your message.

Alternatively, you can make an audio recording as you read your letter. Do this only if you have a quiet recording environment and a quality recording device. (Some MP3 players have this capability.) Be sure to speak and read expressively. Rehearse until you're comfortable with every nuance in the letter. If you wish, you can later edit the recordings using free or low-cost audio-editing software.

Letters aren't the only way to express appreciation. The possibilities are limited only by your imagination! Here are a few ideas:

Create an audio or video recording. Talk lovingly in a video or audio recording, speaking from the heart as best you can. Ideally, you've memorized your key points but you can occa-sionally refer to notes off camera. You can rig a teleprompter for your notes, using either a computer screen or large-print cards managed by a friend. (Follow the additional advice noted in previous paragraphs of this chapter about video and audio recordings.)

After you've finishing recording, place each video or audio recording on its own DVD or CD and label it attractively. If the recording stands alone, present it in the way you feel most comfortable. You can also present it with your heartfelt letter.

Do you write poetry? Write an original poem that focuses on your history with the person you're writing to. End it by expressing your sincere appreciation. You can package and present your poem in a way similar to how you would package and present a letter. (Follow the advice noted earlier in Part 1.)

Do you create fine art? Express how you feel graphically. You can assemble several pencil or pen-and-ink drawings to illustrate the points you want to make. If you're a cartoonist, you can create one or more cartoon strips to convey your points. If you're a photographer or scrapbooker, you can assemble a photo collage showing treasured times with the one you're writing to. Use the art you enjoy.

Do you compose songs? Your original music and lyrics can artistically convey your feelings of appreciation. You can present the music in the form of sheet music. You can sing and record the song you wrote, then create a CD. Similarly, you can produce a DVD in which you perform your song. If you like this idea but feel unprepared to do it yourself, hire a composer/performer to help you. You'll still accomplish your goal of creatively delivering a heartfelt message to the person you care about.

PART 2

WRITING FOR SPECIAL OCCASIONS

BIRTHDAYS

You can't help getting older,
but you don't have to get old.

—George Burns

Most cultures throughout the world like to celebrate people's birthdays—usually with a birthday card, often with a gift, and sometimes with a party. But you can give the best, most long-lasting gift of all when you write a letter explaining why you're grateful to know the birthday honoree. This chapter highlights the birthdays most people consider extra special, because they are ideal times to write a heartfelt letter.

PREGNANCY AND BIRTH

Whether it's a first child or a tenth, a baby's arrival into the world is among the most special of occasions enjoyed by the baby's parents, grandparents, brothers, sisters, aunts, uncles, and friends. New babies represent exciting changes in the lives of those who love them!

If you're expectant parents, there's nothing like that first moment when you discover you're expecting a baby. You feel awe at the miracle of life, coupled with a sense of responsibility providing for that life and helping your child reach its potential.

At a time like this, what a treasure it can be to write a letter to your spouse or partner, expressing confidence that he or she will be a great parent. Just two of the many ways to honor the occasion would be to present your letter over a candlelit dinner or on a picnic in the woods.

You can also write a letter to your unborn child, sharing your hopes and dreams for a great future. Be sure to take care that your language places no limits on your child's potential. Don't hesitate to journal your thoughts as a parent during the pregnancy and express your experience the day your child is born. With each entry you write, you can mention how old the baby is in terms of prenatal weeks. Once your child is old enough to appreciate it, you can read aloud from this journal—just to your child—as a way to show your love. Imagine how treasured that journal will be when you present it as a gift to your child at a later time—perhaps when he or she marries or becomes a parent, too.

Remember your baby's big brothers and sisters, too, at this special time. When hearing of the pending new arrival, they may have mixed feelings: concern about sharing their parents' attention; excitement at being the "big brother" or "big sister" who can show the little one about life; even enthusiasm at someday having a new playmate. A few months or weeks before the baby is born, write personal letters to each of your children. Express gratitude for who they are as individuals; explain the important role they will play in the baby's life and in the newly expanded family; convey confidence they will make you proud as they carry new family responsibilities; remark that the baby will be very lucky to have him or her as a sibling. You can add colorful stickers to your younger children's letters. Then roll up the letters and tie each one with a ribbon. To make your child feel special, present and read this letter to him or her privately, away from the other children. If your child is old enough, entrust him or her with the letter's safekeeping. Otherwise, store it in a safe place. Occasionally bring it out and read it again.

This is a perfect time, too, to write a letter to your own parents—the soon-to-be grandparents—to acknowledge and thank them for raising you as they have. You can describe the parental values you've learned from them and plan to emulate when you become a parent.

Once your baby is born, you'll experience a renewed sense of wonder when you gaze into your child's eyes and see your baby gaze back with total innocence and trust. Yes, your life will suddenly be busy, but think ahead. By taking time to write a letter to your little one now, you'll be leaving a genuine treasure for your baby in later years. Share your deepest thoughts and feelings at this momentous occasion.

If you're a grandparent, hearing "the big news" makes you reflect on the continuity of life through the generations. It can evoke a sense of pride in a job well done raising your own child—an adult about to embark on the same exciting journey of parenthood you and your spouse traveled together. What a great time to write a letter to the soon-to-be new parents. Tell them how excited you are, describe how much you have always loved and appreciated them, and express your confidence that they'll make great parents.

Also write letters to the baby's older brothers and sisters (for ideas, see the suggestions for expectant parents), adding your unique perspective and feelings as Grandma or Grandpa.

Finally, once you meet the new arrival, you can write a special letter to the little one, sharing your feelings and hopes for the future. Ask the baby's parents to save this letter and put it in a safe place as a treasured heirloom.

Brothers and sisters, as a follow up to receiving their parents' letters of gratitude and hope for the future, might even be encouraged by their parents to write their own letters to their unborn baby brother or sister. Here, age-appropriate ideas can be expressed, and your children can add stickers or color pictures to go with what they've written. If your children are too young to write the letters themselves, offer to jot down what they say. And remember the parent's journal? Your children can also be encouraged to journal their thoughts about their new sibling, both before and after the baby is born.

15ᵀᴴ BIRTHDAY: QUINCEAÑERA

In Latin countries and cultures, this 15th birthday of a teen-age girl traditionally marks the transition from child to young woman. In Mexico, for example, the girl wears elegant makeup and a formal evening dress or ball gown. In some countries, the celebration has religious overtones, perhaps beginning with a Thanksgiving mass in which the girl wears a formal dress of pink or white to symbolize the treasured quality of purity.

It's easy to envision parents, grandparents, brothers, sisters, even aunts and uncles writing a letter of congratulations to the honoree, who is sometimes called the Quinceañera. In such a letter, they can write about seeing the young girl growing up, describing her best qualities, giving examples of when she exhibited those traits, and then expressing best wishes for her bright future as a young woman.

16ᵀᴴ BIRTHDAY

Ah, sweet sixteen! For girls, especially, this birthday marks a special time in life. Whether it means having permission to date, soon being able to drive, or simply feeling closer to womanhood, it's an ideal birthday for you—her parents—to commemorate by writing a letter she will treasure forever.

If you're writing the letter jointly, begin with an affectionate salutation followed by a paragraph of appreciation from both of you. This may include a fond recollection of the day your daughter was born, expressing the joy you both felt; it may highlight other special memories you'd like to share. (You'll find more ideas at the end of the Family chapter under Ideas for Writing to Your Son or Daughter.) Then include a paragraph from Dad followed by a paragraph from Mom.

Finish the letter with a paragraph from the two of you together, expressing pride in your daughter and confidence in the great future ahead of her. If you write separate letters to her, make them similar in length to convey equal status.

Whether you write or type your letters, use nice stationery in a pretty pastel. Either frame your letter or put it in a matching envelope with the person's name on it. If the contents of your letter are highly personal, present it privately yet with a sense of ceremony, perhaps choosing a special setting such as a gazebo at a nearby public garden. If you know your daughter wouldn't mind having her friends read the letter at a birthday party, present it there instead; you could even read the letter aloud to her and her guests—if she agrees, of course.

18ᵀᴴ BIRTHDAY

This is it—18!—the magic age when children are legally considered adults. They can sign contracts, serve on juries, and vote. They are now legally liable for the consequences of their own actions. What a great opportunity for parents to write a birthday letter honoring their son or daughter!

What might you, as parents, write in a joint letter to your son or daughter? The theme would be responsibility, written in an upbeat manner. You could, for example, briefly chronicle times past when your child behaved responsibly or admirably, perhaps by demonstrating strong ethics, generosity, or kindness toward others, to name but a few circumstances. Then you could transition to the present and thank your young adult for continuing to be a valued member of the family. You could express confidence that the best is yet to come. You know your son or daughter will continue to be an asset to the family as well as to untold others during his or her lifetime. (You'll find more ideas at the end of the Family chapter under Ideas for Writing to Your Son or Daughter.)

And you could close with a wish for every blessing and success in the years to come. Craft this letter carefully; it's sure to be saved and reread over the years.

Use nice stationery with a matching envelope—or a large envelope if you don't want to fold the letter. If you aren't typing the letter and both parents' handwriting is legible, you could each write alternating paragraphs within the letter.

How do you present it? With ceremony, of course! Think of a special, even meaningful setting where both parents can be present for a private presentation. Or, if the letter's contents are such that your son or daughter wouldn't mind having them read aloud or known by friends, then make the presentation at a birthday party—if you're invited, that is!

21ST BIRTHDAY

So much can happen by a 21st birthday. Your young adult could be living away from home (nearby or far away) or still be living with the family. He or she could be attending college, serving in the military, married, working full time, already a parent, or some combination of these. One thing doesn't change, though: It's the bond you have as a family. And the 21st birthday provides a huge opportunity to express it.

By this time, you're beginning to have a better idea of where your son or daughter's long-term interests lie. Use your joint letter to reflect on what your now-adult child's life has meant to you so far, describing a treasured memory or two in the process. (You'll find more ideas at the end of the Family chapter under Ideas for Writing to Your Son or Daughter.) Then look to the present, acknowledging his or her current interests and hopes for the future in a career, in personal relationships, and in making a difference in the world. Offer your support for helping those hopes become reality. And then express your love.

The way you present your letter may be limited or dictated (to some degree) by your 21-year-old's present circumstances. If he or she lives with you or nearby and is single, then a private presentation during a special occasion at home or at a restaurant may be appropriate. If your child is serving in the military or lives far away, your letter could be read aloud over the phone or in a real-time online video session—complete with webcam—and then delivered by mail.

30ᵀᴴ, 40ᵀᴴ, OR 50ᵀᴴ BIRTHDAY

People have traditionally dreaded *these* particular milestone birthdays. And it's no wonder! "Over the hill" and unwanted aging are often primary themes conveyed in humorous greeting cards and snide remarks in supposed honor of these birthdays. Good news, though. You can transform these birthdays into reasons to celebrate—thanks to the positive thoughts conveyed in a simple letter of appreciation.

If your parent is celebrating a birthday, you can mention specific treasured memories in your letter, if space permits. Was one vacation together especially memorable? Why? Is this person a great cook? What stands out in your home cooking or dining experience? Did the two of you ever build or cook something together? How did that go? Did you two ever pursue any sports activities together? If there was a family business and you were involved, what did that teach you? Did you sing songs or play instruments together? Does a particular song bring to mind a funny, joyful, or loving situation between the two of you?

What leisure activities—picnics, camping, boating, reading, golfing, bike riding, plays, musicals, games, sports, amusement parks—have brought you closer together? What made these experiences special to you? Did you take any road trips or Sunday drives together? What were those like? What kind of positive memories do you have?

If you're the adult son or daughter of a parent celebrating a birthday, you could also write about the parenting techniques he or she demonstrated. Was tough love or gentle persuasion applied? Did your parent make you a partner in decision making or discipline? Was he or she quietly firm, confident, or understanding? Was a system of rewards and consequences used? Was gross exaggeration used to make a point? Did your parent put a strong emphasis on education?

Choose to write about how his or her main parenting techniques benefited you growing up. Did a particular disciplinary action from your father or mother make you a better person today? What one-on-one shared times or events did you enjoy together? For example, you may recall learning to read books or the Sunday comics together, camping, playing catch, building a go-cart, or playing checkers or a favorite card game and "getting to win." What emphasis was placed on education while you were growing up? Did your parent insist that you get good grades and go to college? Did he or she help you with your homework or volunteer in your school activities?

Describe the important life lessons your parent taught you. Examples could include boundaries, friendship, integrity, generosity, moral standards, or appropriate behaviors. How will your future be better because of your parent's influence? *This can be the strongest part of your letter.* (Find more ideas on what to write under Ideas for Writing to Your Parents, located near the end of the Family chapter.)

If you're the spouse or significant other of the celebrant, your letter will focus on your life experiences together. What was life like in the early years of your relationship? If you have children, how did that change the dynamic of your relationship? How did he or she grow, as a parent or stepparent? Did you overcome a major challenge together? How did he or she come through for you at that time?

Was there a particular vacation together that you hold dear in your memory? What made it special? What sports, hobbies, or other recreational activities do the two of you enjoy together? Were any of these introduced to you by him or her? What have the two of you learned about relationships as you've grown older together? How has he or she contributed to the success of your relationship today?

Presenting this letter will depend on whether there's a party and on whether the letter's contents are intended to remain private and personal, rather than shared with others. But either way, deliver your letter personally, if you can.

80ᵀᴴ, 90ᵀᴴ, OR 100ᵀᴴ BIRTHDAY

Most people in their later years have led active lives and are now changing gears: taking time to enjoy their grandchildren and great-grandchildren, perhaps engaging in a few volunteer activities, spending more time on hobbies, and certainly reminiscing about the past and the people they've met and experiences they've had in their full, rich lives.

There's no better time than one of these later milestone birthdays to write a letter expressing your gratitude for who they are and the part they've played in your life. Such a letter helps bring meaning to a life well lived, and the honoree will read your letter again and again. And someday, after he or she has died, descendants will appreciate that letter too, as your description of their loved one adds to the depth of their knowledge and appreciation of their ancestor.

If you're a brother, sister, son, daughter, niece, nephew, grandchild, or great-grandchild of the honoree, examine your unique relationship. What special qualities do you note and admire? What activities did you or do you enjoy together? What memories about the two of you do you especially treasure, and why? In what ways do you aspire to be like him or her?

For example, a woman might write to her father-in-law, describing his unique talents and rare qualities, and then indicate which of these she feels were passed along to her husband. She could tell about childhood memories her husband has shared about his dad and say how much he is loved and appreciated for raising the wonderful man she married: "If a man's success can be measured by how his children turn out, then you, Dad, are the most successful man I know." (Find more ideas on what to write under Ideas for Writing to Your Parents, located near the end of the Family chapter.) The letter can end with a note of congratulations and love, as well as wishes for a long and happy life.

A letter like this lends itself well to a public reading at a birthday celebration. But once again, if distance prevents a personal presentation, your letter can be mailed in a large envelope instead.

SCHOOL

School days, school days
Dear old golden rule days...
—Will D. Cobb

School is a child's first career. It can be a long one, often continuing into a person's 20s and well beyond. When they receive a letter of congratulations, students reaching their own educational milestones will be grateful for the depth it adds to their special occasion. It conveys well-deserved acknowledgment for all they have accomplished and are preparing to accomplish.

FIRST DAY OF KINDERGARTEN

Do you remember your first day of kindergarten? Did one of your parents bring you to school and give you a big hug and kiss? Did he or she tell you to have fun and offer assurance that Mommy or Daddy would pick you up after school? Did you feel afraid you might be forgotten?

Yes, that first day of school can be frightening for a youngster who hasn't been adequately prepared. What if you, as a parent, were to lessen those fears by writing a special letter of appreciation to your child?

Parents, remember you're writing to a young child. Make it a brief, age-appropriate message that you would read aloud to him or her. Perhaps you'd even read it the day before, if not on the morning of the big day.

You can enhance your letter with simple crayon drawings of the two (or three) of you holding hands as a family, each of you with a red heart drawn over your heads. You could depict other kindergartners playing nearby and inviting your child to join them. You can even draw the teacher nearby, smiling and waving, and add other people and objects, too.

Indeed, your entire drawing (or series of drawings) could be your gift of confidence and love to your child. You could present it with spoken words of encouragement about how much fun kindergarten will be. Say how you know your child will make you proud by being a good playmate to the other kindergarteners and getting along well with everyone.

Presenting this letter and/or set of drawings would be ideal if both parents were present, with your child seated between you, each of you with an arm around your little one.

GREAT OR IMPROVED REPORT CARD

As a child, you may recall having had bad grades on your report card and being frightened to present it to your parents for their signature. But the next quarter, your extra effort bore fruit in the form of greatly improved grades. Perhaps you received B's or C's on one report card, yet in the next one, your grades were practically all A's. In either case, the significant improvement can be cause for celebration.

Parents, if your child receives a good report card or shows improvement in some way, remember what it was like for you as a kid. You can certainly reward your child's achievements with money or celebrate with a special activity. In addition, you could cap it with a letter saying how proud you feel about your child. Indeed, your heartfelt letter can serve as the ultimate in positive reinforcement. The letter needn't be long; just express your love and compliment your child on the high achievement that resulted from diligence and hard work. Then tie in the good grades with a note saying how rewarding school can be when students apply themselves—just as he or she has done. Wrap it up by saying you had every confidence he or she could meet the goals set. With your letter, offer your congratulations while continuing to express your love and support.

FIRST DAY OF MIDDLE SCHOOL OR HIGH SCHOOL

Elementary school can be a sheltered place where kids play together and interact in mostly cooperative ways. Middle school, on the other hand, represents the beginning of out-of-control teen hormones, a tough academic workload, and intense peer pressure to conform.

Then high school is typified by those still-raging hormones and a steadily tougher workload. Thankfully, most students exhibit some degree of tolerance for individuals who don't conform. And diverse opportunities to belong are available—in sports, music, clubs, honor societies, volunteer organizations, and student council—all activities providing a kind of warm-up for adulthood. And at some point, of course, dating begins. So many changes occur in only three or four years!

Throughout these times, pre-teens and teens are exploring who they are, defining where they belong, discovering with whom they feel comfortable, and further developing their sense of right and wrong. They're exercising a growing desire for independence. And, yes, sometimes they rebel against their parents.

Parents, all this can be influenced in a positive way when your pre-teen or teen receives a letter from you expressing shared excitement about the upcoming school year while acknowledging added academic and peer pressure. Focus the main part of your letter on your child's positive characteristics. Describe the more admirable key traits and give an example of how the young person exhibited them. Wrap up your letter expressing your confidence and pride in your child's ability to exercise good judgment academically and in all other facets of life. Communicate your knowledge that those positive traits will serve him or her well for a lifetime. And remind your child of your love and that you're always available and ready to help.

HIGH SCHOOL GRADUATION

For most people, a high school diploma culminates a 13-year academic career, but it actually means a lot more. Although graduates are still in their teens, the high school graduation ceremony marks their launch into adulthood.

Whether you're parents, grandparents, or a brother or sister of the graduate, begin your letter by acknowledging an academic job well done. But make your letter more memorable by stating the qualities you've always appreciated in him or her, and perhaps describe a shared memory or two. (Parents: You'll find more ideas at the end of the Family chapter under Ideas for Writing to Your Son or Daughter.) Then conclude your letter by expressing four things: hope for the graduate's future, confidence in his or her ability to rise to the challenges ahead, assurance of moral support whenever needed, and your love.

GOING AWAY TO A COLLEGE DORM OR OTHER NEW LIVING QUARTERS

Changes abound! For parents, this "moving" occasion may mark the onset of ENS—Empty Nest Syndrome. For brothers and sisters, it means the end of a household family dynamic they've known most or all of their lives.

You, as parents, can take this opportunity to remind your young adult of your love. You can also offer sage advice (but not *too* much of it) that you learned when you first left your own childhood home. Be sure to express once again the traits you admire in him or her. As well, mention the specific positive traits that will come in handy as your maturing child learns to live independently. (Find more ideas at the end of the Family chapter under Ideas for Writing to Your Son or Daughter.) You can allude to a poignant shared memory from his or her early childhood; then contrast it with your fledgling's sprouting wings and embarking on a grand adventure alone. Close your letter with an expression of your love and ongoing moral support.

If you're a younger brother or sister to the young adult leaving home, you may be having mixed feelings. Sure, you'll gain more personal living space, but you'll also be losing a longtime confidant *or* a friendly rival. Go ahead. Put your thoughts into a letter that your big brother or sister will treasure. Reminisce about the good times you've shared. Say what a great role model your older brother or sister has been to you. Describe the positive traits he or she has that you want to emulate. Mention that even though you might be gaining bigger living quarters, the space seems empty without him or her. Wish your big brother or sister every success on the new adventure away from home. Close your letter by stating your love and sharing hope that the two of you will keep in close touch.

UNDERGRADUATE OR GRADUATE DEGREE OR CERTIFICATION

Earning a college degree takes longer to achieve these days than a decade or two ago. Classes fill up fast; the cost of tuition and books are budgeted over a long period. Adding to this may be the personal challenges under which the educational goal is being achieved. Perhaps the student has to work part time or full time to help the family or even start a new family, thus sacrificing aspects of a social life.

With so many demands on resources—time, finances, emotions, and so on—holding things together can be a challenge. So when a student has persevered and completed a certificate program or earned an associate, bachelor's, master's, or doctorate degree, the achievement merits your admiration. It's definitely a reason to write the student a letter of congratulations.

If you're parents of the graduate, discuss your firsthand observation of the dedication your graduate has shown along the way. Tell about the qualities that served him or her well, and express your hopes for the future, whether it involves continuing classes to earn the next academic degree or entering a new career. And of course, end the letter by expressing your ongoing love and support.

If you're the graduate's brother or sister, express admiration for the graduate's achievement and appreciation for the role model the graduate has represented in your own life. Also describe particular attributes you admire and want to emulate. Then end with an affectionate comment.

If you're the graduate's spouse, you can also write about sacrifices, but be careful. Tell about the sacrifices the graduate has made along the way, but avoid a martyr-like laundry list of the sacrifices you or the rest of the family have had to make. Instead, allude to the fact that the various sacrifices made by you and other family members were investments you felt honored to make toward this wonderful achievement. Describe the admirable qualities you see in the graduate. Then end the letter with an expression of your love and devotion.

MILITARY

Let us have faith that right makes might, and in that faith let us to the end dare to do our duty as we understand it.

—Abraham Lincoln

The major military service branches in the U.S. are the Army, Marine Corps, Navy, Air Force, and Coast Guard, as well as the Reserve and National Guard divisions of each. Enlistees' terms of service can vary from 3 to 6 years, depending on the branch and other circumstances. Recruits within each major branch begin with 6 to 13 weeks of basic training, usually followed by advanced training that can take from 2 weeks to a year.

After advanced training, the service member's duty assignment begins. If that assignment takes place in a combat zone, the service member stays 6 months or a year unless he or she is serving in a permanent capacity (e.g., as an officer). In some branches, after a yearlong period at the home station, service members sometimes elect to return to the combat zone for another term. This is followed by another return to the home station for the remainder of the tour of duty.

BASIC TRAINING AND GRADUATION
All military recruits, whether drafted or enlisted, begin their service with at least a 6- to 8-week basic training. During this time, they acquire the basic tools needed to develop their

bodies, minds, and emotions to a state appropriate for serving in the military.

Recruits are encouraged to prepare for basic training by sticking to a schedule and exercising regularly. They're advised to delegate personal affairs to family or friends so they can maintain their focus on training and, later, military service. Basic training makes recruits strong and capable so by the time they graduate, they're able to carry out orders quickly and efficiently.

During times of war or other military action, it's natural for new recruits to feel anxiety about the danger they might face in their tour of duty. Even during peacetime, recruits often feel anxious when thinking about how the military will change their lives. For these reasons, a busload of recruits heading to basic training might be rather subdued. On the other hand, as basic training ends, recruits feel both relief and a sense of achievement at having completed the first hurdle on their military path.

If you're writing to a recruit who will soon begin basic training, be supportive of the recruit's decision to join the military. While it's okay to admit you'll miss him or her, express your confidence that he or she will learn a lot and perform well. Acknowledge the many valuable, life-changing experiences that couldn't be acquired in any other way. Convey the traits you've always valued in him or her. Also say how much you look forward to seeing the new person who will emerge from this experience. Then end with a note expressing your affection or friendship.

If you're writing to a recruit already enrolled in basic training, do so regularly. At the end of that first month of basic training, the recruit is adapting to military life. Still, the schedule is grueling, beginning well before sunrise and ending only after dinner. Remember, despite the recruit's aching body and probable exhaustion, letters from home always provide a welcome respite. So when you write, give upbeat reports of life back home while being supportive and encouraging.

If you're writing to a recruit who's just graduated from basic training, you may be lucky enough to deliver that letter in person at the graduation ceremony. This letter will formally congratulate the graduate on a job well done while commenting favorably on how he or she has changed during this important time. Wrap up the letter with your best wishes for the next phase of training.

ACTIVE SERVICE TO ONE'S COUNTRY

During the advanced training period that follows basic training, recruits are getting settled into the military way of life. With a somewhat lighter exercise regimen, the day-to-day atmosphere is more like going to school (which of course it is); therefore, for most, the stress level is lower than during basic training.

During the duty assignment after advanced training, service members—especially those serving in a combat region—can once again experience high stress levels. Depending on the nature of the duty, though, they won't have time to think about it, especially if they're busy doing heavy physical labor. If part of their duty involves dealing with threats and other dangers, the stress they feel can peak.

If you're a family member writing to a service member whose duty circumstances are unknown to you, exercise good judgment in what you say. Be upbeat as you write about what's going on at home, barely mentioning things he or she might worry about. Express assurance that you'll all get by. Mostly convey your pride for his or her serving the country while you show confidence your service member will do well. Mention that you miss him or her and you'll keep thoughts of your service member in your prayers. Send your love and, if it's feasible, promise to send homemade food.

Suggestions for sending food. The United States Postal Service (USPS) is the only U.S. shipping service that will ship to APO, FPO, and DPO military addresses at domestic-shipping rates. They will also supply free Priority Mail shipping supplies for this purpose when you call 800-610-8734 and request the "military pack." For other USPS military shipping guidelines, visit USPS.com/ship/apo-fpo-guidelines.htm. Expect transit time for food packages to be 7 to 10 days.

Package your food inside the box using airtight bags. Foods that service members especially like include beef jerky, candy, instant oatmeal, trail mix, granola and nutrition bars, homemade nut bread, and of course cookies. If there is any question whether the food will keep well in transit or in high-temperature conditions, use thick foam containers and freezer packs (the type used in shipping insulin and other refrigerated medications to diabetic patients, medical offices, and pharmacies).

If you're writing to an unknown service member as part of an appreciation campaign for those in combat duty, always write about upbeat things. Describe the pleasant aspects of your home environment, say what your family is like, mention going to school, making special home-cooked meals, going on picnics, and so on. Then say how much you appreciate living in a country that affords you and your fellow citizens those freedoms. Express your appreciation for the efforts this service member and all the rest are making to help preserve those freedoms.

ABOVE AND BEYOND THE CALL OF DUTY

While serving a tour of duty, your family service member may be recognized with a medal such as the Medal of Honor, Service Cross, or Distinguished Service (including the Silver Star), or a Bronze Star with a V device for valor, for having acted bravely or otherwise having exceeded the call of duty.

Sometimes, the medal awarded is received within four weeks of the action that earned it; other times, it's given in a ceremony after the service member has returned from the combat zone to the home duty station. If the award is given while the person remains in the combat zone, he or she may not be at liberty to discuss it with you for security reasons until after returning to the home duty station. Either way, it's only through the service member that you'll learn of this award. That person could make a short-notice call like this: "Hey, can you come to a ceremony here at the base next Friday? They've told me I'm getting a special award." You probably won't know the specifics of the medal until the ceremony takes place.

If you're a member of the family, once you learn the details about the medal and why it was awarded, your service member will treasure a letter of appreciation from you. In that letter, note that you heard about the wonderful honor and feel proud, but given who he or she is, you're also not surprised. Go on to mention past acts of integrity. Wrap up your letter by asking him or her to take care and keep up the good work. Then, of course, convey that you're sending your prayers and good thoughts. You could even attach a sticky note with a smiley face saying you'll send a batch of celebration cookies soon!

WHEN A SERVICE MEMBER DIES
IN THE LINE OF DUTY

The death of any family member can feel devastating. Yet, it's even more upsetting if that death takes place unexpectedly, such as when members of the military die while performing their duties, usually in a combat zone. *Grief stricken* barely begins to describe what family members feel at this time. Yes, it's thoughtful and necessary to write a letter of condolence, but do so with utmost consideration.

What *not* to write in your condolence letter to the family:

- ◆ "I know what you must be going through."
  You can't possibly know, because grief is unique
  to the individual.

- ◆ "It was God's will." While you may believe this in
  your heart, it isn't at all comforting to the bereaved
  family to read it. Family members may be angry
  with God for allowing their loved one to die.

- ◆ "I'll bet you wish (Name) had never joined the
  military." Saying this only adds to the pain the
  family already feels. It also dishonors the memory
  of the deceased service member who may have
  exercised free will in choosing to join the
  armed forces.

What thoughts *will* be appreciated in your condolence letter:

- ◆ "I'm so sorry for your loss," "I know you must be
  hurting," "We'll all miss (Name)," and other
  traditional thoughts of condolence are always
  appropriate.

- ◆ "Our country has lost a great individual, and so
  have we all."

- ◆ "(Name) was an exceptional service member who
  went above and beyond what was expected."

If you're a close relative or friend of the family, it's also always appropriate to say you're here for the family and ready to assist in any way needed to deal with their loss. And this is important: Remember to check back in a month or so, demonstrating that your offer of help was sincere. Don't wait for them to call you. You might also mark your calendar for the anniversary of the service member's death. Around that time, write a brief letter to the family acknowledging their loss, saying "I miss (Name)," and offering once again to be of assistance in any way you can.

If you're a military or civilian friend of the deceased service member, you'll find the family appreciates not only your condolences but also your mention of several pleasant memories you recall about your friend. Mark your calendar for the anniversary of your friend's death and write a brief letter to family members at that time. In the letter, acknowledge their loss, say you miss your friend, and offer to assist in any way you can.

HONORABLE DISCHARGE

An honorable discharge, the top-ranked military discharge, is awarded to service members who have completed their tour of duty and received a "good to excellent" rating for their service. Customarily, no ceremony is performed when an honorable discharge is given.

But the service member, especially one who served in a combat zone, engages in a sort of mental celebration. No doubt he or she is grateful to return to a safe environment and could even feel a sense of euphoria at having completed the tour of duty—now able to return to civilian life, career, and family.

If you're a friend or family member, you'll find this the perfect time to write the new civilian a letter of appreciation, bringing added "ceremony" to the occasion. The honorable discharge is, after all, cause for celebration and congratulations. Certainly express those sentiments in your letter, but also add substance by thanking the newly discharged individual for defending your country and family. Acknowledge that he or she did something admirable—something few others would have done. You can also thank the new civilian for having stood up for what is right. And finally, you can end with a rousing "Welcome home!"

MILITARY RETIREMENT

In any branch of U.S. military service, service members can retire after 20 years. During the military career, their priorities have been to do what needs to be done and stay out of trouble. Additionally, the service member may take classes at the community college or university level, because the education pay proves useful during their military career or in a civilian career following retirement from the military.

The challenges of a military career are many, the most apparent relating to the frequent relocation of the service member and family. Even though a move is usually preceded by several months' notice, the entire family must be adaptable, ready at any time to pick up roots and move to a new area. They're leaving old friends behind (though often pledging to stay in touch) and then, ideally, taking steps at school or through community involvement to make new friends quickly.

Children in military families sometimes hesitate to form strong friendships after a move, feeling reluctant to lose those friends in the next move. Instead, they form stronger bonds with their siblings; after all, siblings are part of the family that moves every time. Smart service members and their spouses recognize the value of friendship and community. They proactively establish relationships quickly after a move, although they can have more difficulty if they live in a civilian neighborhood where it can sometimes take years to meet one's neighbors. Nevertheless, strong bonds can be established and nurtured with both military and non-military friends from all over the world, thanks to technology— telephone, email, instant messaging, social media, free video calls, and video conferencing—plus traditional letter writing.

The occasional long absences of the service member are another challenge. These times can be lonely for the children as well as the spouse, who must temporarily handle all parenting responsibilities and household management.

It's also true that a military salary is lower than its counterpart in civilian life. However, the following items are also paid by the military:

♦ The service member's meals

♦ The service member's full college tuition

♦ A housing allowance

♦ All military-relocation expenses

♦ Full medical care and prescriptions for the entire family

Considering these benefits, the service member can enjoy a similar lifestyle to that of a civilian who has comparable job responsibilities.

When a service member retires, he or she feels a sense of personal honor and pride, more than anything else, at having accomplished so much during the military career. He or she can reflect on career experiences with a sense of enjoyment and self-fulfillment. At the same time, though, he or she may look on retirement with a sense of trepidation. After all, for 20 years, military life is all the service member has known. What an adjustment it will be to leave that familiar environment and venture into the unknown. The retiree may wonder, "What will I do next?" or "How will things play out?"

In most cases, it means starting a second career in civilian life to stay busy. Certainly, another factor is providing the family with added income if they didn't save or invest well over the years.

The retirement ceremony is a personal highlight in the service member's career. All family members, friends, relatives, superiors, and subordinates who wish to attend are made welcome. The ceremony, which takes place at the home base, lasts a little over an hour. It can be likened to a commencement ceremony for one. Among the awards is a congratulatory letter of appreciation from the President of the United States, presented by a high-ranking officer.

At the ceremony, speeches are made not only by superior officers but also by service members the retiree has mentored and who may soon become successors. Some of those speeches may seem more like "roasts" with lots of friendly ribbing and laughter; but speakers eventually express their respect and admiration. They commend the retiree personally and professionally for a job well done. The retiree, too, makes a farewell speech, publicly acknowledging not only the military service members present but also the support of his or her spouse, family, and friends.

If you're a friend or family member writing a letter of congratulations, you can cite and compliment the retiree on the accomplishments you know took place during the 20-year career. Express your appreciation on a job well done serving the country and in having had a well-thought-out career plan from the start. If you've been able to observe the family and seen that the service member has treated them well, it would be appropriate to compliment that behavior as well.

If you have served with the retiree and are writing a letter of congratulations and appreciation, then everything in the preceding paragraph applies. However, you can elaborate on the retiree's admirable mentorship of other service members who would be succeeding him or her. You may also wish to thank the retiree more personally for being an excellent superior officer, subordinate, mentor, or friend, as the case may be.

If you're a family member or friend wishing to express appreciation, you may either add to your letter of congratulations or write a separate letter of thanks, depending on how private those sentiments will be. *As a spouse,* you may have highly personal thoughts to share about the relationship challenges encountered and overcome during the military career. Or mention several triumphant personal or professional moments when you were particularly proud of your service member.

If you're a child of the retiree, this letter may be an opportunity to describe the values you've observed in your parent about service to country and devotion to family. Perhaps cite an instance when your relationship was tested, and how each of you weathered the experience successfully. Finally, take this opportunity to say thank you and express your pride in being his or her son or daughter.

As a personal friend, you may want to comment on what the friendship has meant to you throughout the years. You can say that seeing military life through the eyes of your friend has brought a different perspective to your life. You may also wish to comment on the values you've observed and admired in your friend during his or her military career—values you have tried to emulate.

VETERANS DAY: HONORING A VETERAN'S SERVICE

Veterans Day is not merely a paid legal holiday; it's a day set aside to honor everyone—living or dead—who has ever served in the U.S. Armed Forces. This day of observance was established in 1919 to celebrate the one-year anniversary of the end of hostilities in World War I. In 1926, Congress made a resolution to observe November 11 with appropriate ceremonies. A congressional act in 1938 made Armistice Day a legal holiday, deeming it a day dedicated to the cause of world peace and celebrated and known as Armistice Day, honoring those who had served in World War I. In May 1954, a bill was signed into law establishing November 11 as Armistice Day, a federal holiday. The following month, Congress amended the act to replace "Armistice" with "Veterans," to more clearly represent all veterans.

Past and present U.S. military personnel in every capacity have sacrificed their personal independence—sometimes their well-being or their lives—to act on behalf of their country and its citizens during their tours of duty. Regardless of U.S.–condoned military actions being considered ill-advised by some of its citizens, this in no way diminishes the gratitude we should all feel *and express* toward those who served. They did their best for their country in compliance with their military orders.

If you know people who served or are currently serving their country—or if you know families of deceased service members—you can participate in making Veterans Day a time of healing by writing heartfelt letters of gratitude.

If you're writing to currently enlisted service members, it's appropriate to say you're thinking of them on Veterans Day and want to thank them for their service. You can say they're

an asset to their family and/or community, and then convey the qualities you appreciate about them.

If you're writing to past service members—even and *especially* those who served in an unpopular military conflict or who suffered a permanent disability because of their service—it's particularly key to thank them. Acknowledge them for their sacrifice and dedication on behalf of their country during their tour of duty. Once again, describe the qualities you appreciate about them, especially the ways in which they're an asset to those around them.

If you're writing to the family of a deceased service member, refer to the suggestions in the next section, Memorial Day, for guidance.

MEMORIAL DAY

Memorial Day in the U.S. originated (and is still observed) as a day of remembrance for those who died in their nation's service. Unfortunately, the purpose of Memorial Day was somewhat obscured when the National Holiday Act of 1971 changed the day of observance from May 30 to the last Monday in May. This created a three-day weekend filled with recreational opportunities but not always observing the purpose intended.

To reinstate its original meaning (as noted on a website dedicated to restoring the traditional day of observance for Memorial Day):

> We need to remember with sincere respect those who paid the price for our freedoms; we need to keep in sacred remembrance those who died serving their country. We need to never let them be forgotten. (USMemorialDay.org/act.html)

In addition to flying the American flag at half-staff on Memorial Day, you can also write to family members of people who died, recently or long ago, while serving their country. Express your gratitude and your condolences.

If you're writing to a family who suffered a recent loss, mention that you're thinking of them on Memorial Day. Refer to the two lists in the earlier section, When a Service Member Dies in the Line of Duty, for guidance regarding what *not* to write and what *will* be appreciated in your letter. You could also add personal recollections regarding the deceased service member, even a description of the service member's finer qualities. Perhaps you could close with the comment that the individual was a credit to the uniform and that, while gone, he or she will never be forgotten. And remind the family that, if you can be of help, you'd like to be asked, because you're here for them.

If you're writing to a family who lost a loved one in the more distant past, it's still appropriate to mention you're thinking of them on Memorial Day. Acknowledge that our country lost a great person; then say you miss (Name) and still think about him or her often. From there, describe pleasant memories and the individual's finest qualities. Close by saying (Name) was a credit to the uniform and will never be forgotten.

ROMANCE

My bounty is as boundless as the sea, my love as deep;
the more I give to thee, the more I have,
for both are infinite.

—William Shakespeare, *Romeo and Juliet*

Whether it's an engagement, marriage, romantic anniversary, romantic holiday, or a romantic "un-occasion," you can enhance your relationship (even an ailing one) by writing and presenting a letter. It can beautifully express your love and your appreciation for the positive aspects of your life together.

ENGAGEMENT

Being engaged to be married is momentous for the couple as well as their families. It's a time to "make sure"—well, as sure as two people in love can hope to be at an early stage. An engagement involves making important decisions about career, living arrangements, children, and more, as well as planning the wedding ceremony itself.

If you're the man or woman who's become engaged, your fiancée or fiancé will be thrilled to receive a special love letter close to the time of the engagement or shortly afterward. You'll find plenty of ideas for what to include under Ideas for Writing a Romantic Letter at the end of this chapter.

If you're the parents of the future bride or groom, you can write a letter of appreciation and love for your daughter or son soon after the announcement is made. In your letter, you can call to mind special memories about when you yourselves were first married and/or when your daughter or son was born. You can select poignant or funny incidents during your daughter or son's childhood to convey. You can also relate the qualities about your son or daughter you most admire—ones that will serve him or her well in the marriage. End the letter with your best wishes and your pledge of love and support. You'll find ideas aplenty under Ideas for Writing to Your Son or Daughter at the end of the Family chapter.

You can also write a heartfelt letter to your future son-in-law or daughter-in-law. Your letter can express your joy and congratulations at being able to welcome him or her into your family. You can convey the person's most admirable traits, especially those you believe will serve him or her well in the marriage. End your letter with the hope that he or she will think of you as a second set of loving parents—a cheerleading team—throughout a long, joyful, and rewarding marriage.

If you're the brother or sister of the future bride or groom, start with congratulations and say how thrilled you are with your brother or sister's choice in a future spouse, mentioning the qualities you especially like in your future sister- or brother-in-law. Then describe the qualities you especially admire in your newly engaged brother or sister. Tell about your own special relationship with him or her, emphasizing what you've always treasured. End with the idea that even though you know the dynamics of your relationship will soon change, you're always here for your sibling, and that you'll treasure the times together as an expanded family.

If you're a good friend of the future bride or groom, first congratulate your friend and then describe the qualities you especially like and/or admire about the person he or she has chosen to marry. Relate some wonderful times you and your friend have enjoyed together; then describe the qualities of your friend that you admire most. Also say you recognize that, with marriage, your friend will have a new "best friend forever" (BFF), but you know that you and he or she will continue to treasure your friendship well into the future. End by saying you know you'll always be there for each other.

MARRIAGE

When two people vow to remain together for the rest of their lives, from that moment forward almost nothing is as it was. It's no wonder that people consider marriage the most life-changing occasion of all. Surrounding this ceremony are many superb opportunities to write letters of appreciation—to the bride, the groom, and their parents—as the following examples show.

If you're writing to your bride or groom, you can start with how your relationship developed, mentioning specific treasured memories. You can further describe how your relationship has affected your life; then share how you see yourselves building a life together. *Make this the strongest part of your letter.* And if one or both of you have special circumstances, express your feelings on these matters. You'll find plenty of ideas on each of these themes under Ideas for Writing a Romantic Letter at the end of this chapter.

Sweeten your letter by occasionally starting a paragraph with your loved one's name, followed by a comma (e.g., "Cameron, we have so much in common.").

How will you present your letter? Most certainly present your letter in private. After all, its intimate contents are intended for the most important person you'll ever know—the one you want to spend the rest of your life with!

If you're a bride or groom writing to your own parents, think about the many values and life lessons they taught you. Your letter can start with a general paragraph reminiscing about family memories you especially treasure. Then you can write a paragraph to your mom, describing what you value about your relationship and what special lessons you've learned or qualities you've adopted from her. Do the same in a separate paragraph for your dad. In your final paragraph, recap the overall values you've learned that you'll bring into your marriage. End by expressing your appreciation and your love for your parents.

You may consider including points about the parenting techniques they have demonstrated over the years. Also describe the important life lessons your parents taught you. *Make this the most powerful part of your letter.* Mention specific treasured memories, if space permits. And if you're writing to parents who have special circumstances, remember to express your feelings on these matters. You'll find plenty of specific ideas on each of these themes under Ideas for Writing to Your Parents near the end of the next chapter, Family.

How will you present your letter? Consider presenting it, framed, at your rehearsal dinner or in a more private setting with just your parents. If it feels right, include your future spouse, too.

If you're parents writing to your son or daughter getting married, first quietly alert the future in-laws about your surprise gift; they may appreciate the opportunity to surprise their own child with a treasured letter, too.

If a paragraph is intended to be from only one parent, start the paragraph by identifying the writer. For example, "From Dad" can appear on the line above that parent's paragraph(s), followed by a dash ("From Dad—") or a comma ("From Dad,"). Alternatively, the parent's name can appear on the same line as the next sentence, followed by a comma ("Richard, it's Dad. I'll always remember...").

Mention specific treasured memories, if space permits. If your son or daughter deals with special circumstances, remember to express your feelings on these matters. (Under Ideas for Writing to Your Son or Daughter at the end of the next chapter, Family, you'll find suggestions to spark your thinking.)

Recall times when your child showed signs of growing up and what you thought about them. Examples might be when he or she used good judgment in a situation, repaired something major around the house, or showed adult behavior that filled you with pride. Describe times you felt especially pleased with your child, like when a teacher or another parent said something nice, or when your child once told you something insightful.

Describe the growing friendship and love you see between your child and his or her intended. Has their relationship been humorous, dynamic, touching? Can their unique qualities be transformed into building blocks to create a good marriage? Offer your observations.

Be sure to acknowledge the positive qualities of your child's fiancée or fiancé. Mention the qualities that endear her or him to you; point out those that make the two of them well suited to each other. Speak about your hopes for wonderful new family relationships. Describe how you'd like to involve the newlyweds in family activities yet also give them independence to build their own family traditions.

Explain the important life lessons you hope you have imparted to your child. Examples include boundaries, friendship, integrity, generosity, moral standards, appropriate behaviors, the value of a good education, and more. How will the future for your child and his or her spouse be better because of what you have taught? *Make this the strongest part of your letter.*

Reveal lessons you've learned in your own marriage. These may be humorous ("A frying pan is not a birthday present"), supportive ("Care about what your wife or husband is thinking or feeling"), insightful ("You *marry* your [husband/wife]; you don't *control* [him/her]"), and so on.

Offer your suggestions, kept to a minimum, for a healthy marriage. Topics can include trust, respect, friendship, generosity, communication, forgiveness, unconditional love, the Golden Rule, quality time together, or interest in one another's hobbies.

End your letter with a compliment, then close it with whatever wording seems most natural (e.g., "With love," "Affectionately," or "Your loving parents,") followed by a comma. Capitalize only the first word. Then, on the line below, each of you will handwrite the name your child calls you (e.g., "Dad" or "Pop," or "Mom," "Mamma," or "Ma").

If you'd like to choose a theme, look for ideas in the Write It chapter in Part 1.

After writing your heartfelt letter together as parents, you may have questions about what to do next. Frequently asked questions are:

Q. *What should our letter look like?*

A. For a joint presentation from both sets of parents, both letters should appear similar—for example, two framed one-page letters or two ribbon-tied scrolls. Otherwise, any appropriate, respectful treatment will do.

Q. *When is the best time to present our letter?*

A. It depends. Is the other set of parents also writing a letter of appreciation to their son or daughter? If not, then present your letter in private, with only your child present. But if there will be two letters—

one from each set of parents—you and the other parents can plan a joint presentation ceremony.

Q. *Where should the joint presentation take place?*

A. It depends, in part, on the level of privacy desired by both sets of parents. The most private ceremony involves only the future bride and groom and both sets of parents (e.g., at a special dinner a few days before the wedding). On the other hand, the rehearsal dinner is almost as intimate, shared only with your child's closest friends and relatives. The most public of the three options is holding the presentation during the wedding reception. It becomes part of the program and gives the guests meaningful insights into the bride and groom.

Q. *How should the joint presentation take place?*

A. Even at a private ceremony, be sure you and your spouse stand as you read the letter to your son or daughter. At the rehearsal dinner, have your child stand beside you as you read. At the wedding reception, both parents move to the front and you ask your child to stand beside you as you read. In both scenarios, take turns as parents reading appropriate paragraphs. Read only brief excerpts of a long letter so guests don't become impatient— and so your son or daughter doesn't become embarrassed.

Q. *What other enhancements can we add to the experience?*

A. If framed letters were presented before the wedding day to both the bride and groom by their respective parents, then consider displaying them in the foyer near the guest book. That way, guests can read them if they wish before they're seated for the ceremony. Or if your letter of appreciation is being presented in private, you can enhance the experience by also presenting something that both you and the couple value (e.g., a collection of recipes of your child's favorite home-cooked meals).

ROMANTIC ANNIVERSARIES

Many romantic anniversaries can be commemorated with a letter of appreciation and love. Whether you're writing to your significant other, your fiancé/fiancée, your spouse, or your parents (for their own celebration), know that your letter's recipient(s) will treasure that letter always.

If you're writing to commemorate your own romantic anniversary (other than a wedding anniversary), choose from several possible occasions, e.g., a 6-month or 1-year anniversary of your first date; a 6-month, 1-year, or multi-year anniversary of having an exclusive relationship; or a 6-month anniversary of your engagement. You'll find plenty of guidance and inspiration for your anniversary love letter under Ideas for Writing a Romantic Letter at the end of this chapter. Remember, writing this letter is always worth the effort, because your lover will likely treasure it forever.

If you're writing to celebrate your own wedding anniversary, congratulations! Wedded-bliss anniversaries typically take place at 1 month, 6 months, and 1 year. Then, as you settle into a long-lasting marriage, although you'll observe every anniversary, you'll especially celebrate your 5th, 10th, and 25th anniversaries. With continued commitment and longevity, you'll be able to celebrate your milestone 50th and even 75th wedding anniversaries.

At any or all of these occasions—or even every year, as some couples do—you add meaning whenever you give treasured letters to one another celebrating your love. To stimulate ideas, refer to Ideas for Writing a Romantic Letter at the end of this chapter.

If you're writing to your parents to celebrate their special wedding anniversary, you're a wonderful son or daughter; your parents are lucky to have you. This is a great time to tell them how much they mean to you, how much you admire them, and how grateful you are that they've stayed together through good times and bad. You'll find guidance and inspiration for writing your parents' anniversary letter in Ideas for Writing to Your Parents near the end of the next chapter, Family.

VALENTINE'S DAY

Valentine's Day has been made almost too easy—a card, flowers, and chocolates for her, and a card and favorite dinner for him, right? But you can do *so* much better than that. You can shine brightly in your lover's eyes by writing a heartfelt love letter. It will far outlast the cards, flowers, chocolates, and dinner.

For a wealth of guidance and inspiration in writing your Valentine's Day letter, read Ideas for Writing a Romantic Letter at the end of this chapter. When you present your special letter, your lover will appreciate you even more and likely treasure your letter always.

NEW YEAR'S EVE

Many couples write letters to one another every New Year's Eve or New Year's Day. If you'd like to begin this tradition, start your letter with a review of your past year together. Describe your positive perceptions on what has transpired for the two of you, including how you may have overcome challenges together. Then comment on your hopes for the coming year and beyond. And, of course, end your letter by affirming your ongoing love.

Be sure to save all your letters. Reading them together, in succession, makes a wonderful way to review your life together on special anniversaries. In fact, reading old letters before composing a current letter provides context and adds depth as you write your latest New Year's letter.

MORE AMORE (ITALIAN FOR LOVE)

The special relationship enjoyed by you and your fiancé or fiancée, spouse, or lover may be rather new—or decades old. But your relationship never has to *feel* old.

From time to time, think "More *Amore*." In the gaps between your wedding anniversary and Valentine's Day, spice up your love by writing and presenting a letter. Declare, in the most expressive way you can, your love and devotion, as well as your appreciation for the one who shares your life.

IDEAS FOR WRITING A ROMANTIC LETTER

In this section, you'll find a wealth of ideas on what to include when you're writing to that special someone in your life—whether it's for your engagement, your marriage, a special anniversary, Valentine's Day, or another occasion celebrating "More *Amore*."

How did your relationship develop? How did you two first meet? Were you impressed with each other at first sight? What first attracted you to him or her? In the beginning, what was your best date together? Why? What was your most romantic moment together? What was it like for you the first time he or she said "I love you"? How did you first know you were meant to be together? What does it feel like when you're apart? What has typified your relationship so far? What benefits do these characteristics bring to your life together?

You can mention specific treasured memories, space permitting. These questions may spark fond memories for you: What especially fun time(s) have you enjoyed together? What was your most embarrassing moment together? Did the two of you ever build or cook something together? How did that go? Did you sing songs or play instruments together? Does a particular song evoke a funny, joyful, or loving situation between you? What leisure activities—picnics, camping, boating, reading, golfing, bike riding, plays/musicals, games or gaming, sports, amusement parks—have brought you closer together as a couple? What made these experiences special to you? Have you taken any day trips or extended road trips together? What were those like as a couple? What kind of positive memories do you have from them? Do you want to allude to any secrets or inside jokes you share?

You can describe how your relationship has affected your life. For example: How are the two of you most alike or most different? What qualities do you most admire about him or her? What do your family and friends especially like about him or her? What is he or she best known for among your friends? Did the two of you experience any hardships? If so, how did you overcome them? How does he or she respond in a crisis—with efficiency, selflessness, considered action, something else? How have *you* become a better person because of him or her? Has he or she "opened doors" for you, thus enhancing your life? How? How has your loved one become a better person because of you? Why is that so? What positive effect has he or she had on your life? What positive effect have you had on his or her life? What special quality do *you* possess that you believe your loved one values most, either now or in your future together? How comfortable are you around one another? Can you "be yourselves" together? How can you further express why you appreciate your loved one?

62 How to Write Heartfelt Letters to Treasure

Share how you see yourselves building or continuing to build a life together. Tell about friendship, partnership, being stronger as a couple than alone, and achieving dreams together. What is it about the two of you that best indicates your future happiness and success together? In what way will you (or do you) appreciate being with your loved one? *Make this the strongest part of your letter.*

Do you and your loved one have special circumstances? Let the suggestions in the categories that follow spark your thinking about what you would like to write. Remember to express *your* feelings on these matters.

> *Were you childhood sweethearts?* Mention your earliest romantic memory of him or her; indicate that your marriage or your continuing life together is the culmination of a longtime dream.

> *Were you friends long before you started dating each other?* Perhaps mention that first knowing one another as friends has allowed you to appreciate one another as individuals. Add that the more recent, loving relationship you share has become "the icing on the cake." Express hope that your friendship will be one of your strongest bonds, carrying you through life together.

The following special circumstances relate specifically to an upcoming marriage.

> *Are you soon to be part of an arranged marriage?* If so, pledge your full commitment to him or her and to your marriage, expressing sincere hopes for a happy future together.

> *Was one or both of you previously married?* Acknowledge that helpful learning experiences probably came from the previous marriage, and that you're glad to be making a lifetime commitment with him or her now.

Do you have children but he or she doesn't? Express appreciation that your loved one is willing to become part of an instant family, and that you know he or she will become an excellent role model for your children.

If your children are old enough, you may want to write each of them a special letter on the occasion of your marriage. Pledge to continue being a good parent and express confidence that your spouse will do his or her best to be a good stepfather or stepmother.

Does he or she have children but you don't? Write that you are honored to have been asked to be a member of your loved one's family. Say that while you'd never expect to replace the mother or father of his or her children, you will commit to be a good, loving step-parent. Pledge that you will help them enjoy their childhood and grow into young adults who will make you both proud.

If the children are old enough, write each of them a special letter, pledging to be a good spouse to their father or mother and a loving stepparent to them.

Do you both have children? Write that you and your children are honored to have been accepted as part of the family. As you establish your blended family, you welcome the new stepparent and his or her children into your family. Assure your loved one you will strive to be a good stepparent, just as you know he or she will be a good one, too. Pledge that you will face any challenges with love, understanding, and support.

Ultimately, you want to help all the children enjoy their childhood and grow into young adults who will make both of you proud. If your respective children are old enough, you and your groom or bride may each want to write letters to the other's children. Pledge to be a good spouse to their parent and a

good and loving stepparent to them. Remember
to write to your own children, too!

Are either of you or both of you widowed? In your letter,
choose from the following list of ideas and include
whatever applies to you and inspires you.

- ♦ You've been privileged to learn, firsthand,
  how a good partnership helps make a
  good marriage.

- ♦ Your previous marriage helped you
  develop into someone who appreciates
  commitment, care, and compassion.

- ♦ You understand and honor the
  experiences and memories from the
  previous marriage.

- ♦ You're glad to have found your loved one
  now; the two of you are embarking on a
  wonderful journey as a couple.

- ♦ You look forward to sharing the rest of
  your lives together in an equally joyous
  and satisfying way.

FAMILY

Families are the compass that guide us. They are the inspiration to reach great heights, and our comfort when we occasionally falter.

—Brad Henry

This chapter focuses on specific holidays that honor parents and grandparents. It also features ideas for writing to your parents, followed by ideas for writing to your children at different milestones in their lives.

MOTHER'S DAY

Mother's Day is celebrated in more than 40 countries, usually on the second Sunday in May. Its purpose is to honor mothers and the bonds of motherhood. On this day, families want Mom to feel special for her nurturing and her hard work throughout the year.

You can make Mother's Day extra special by supplementing the traditional flowers and candy with a special letter of appreciation. Suggestion: If you're writing to your mother, tell your siblings your plan well in advance of the holiday, so they will have an opportunity to write their own letters if they wish.

What to write in your letter. Say you're thinking of her with fondness on this special day. Describe treasured memories that demonstrate her warmth, love, and dedication to her family.

If you're writing to your wife or partner, say what you've appreciated about her early in your relationship, and what you especially appreciate today about her parenting. Convey her values you most admire; thank her for the positive example she has set for your own behavior and for that of your children. End your letter by expressing hope for a long life together. Be sure to openly profess your love.

If you're writing to your mother, explain what you appreciated about her when you were a child, and what you especially appreciate about her today. You may want to mention memories that demonstrate hard lessons she had to teach you. Tell about the values you've learned from her—those you've already adopted or plan to adopt. Describe how your relationship has matured as you have grown, saying what it's like today. You can find more ideas on what to write under Ideas for Writing to Your Parents, later in this chapter. End your letter by thanking her for the love and support she has always shown you, and then express your ongoing love for her.

How to present your letter. Ideas for framing or presenting your letter abound in the Part 1 chapter Present It. Try to present it in person. If you have siblings who don't have letters of their own to present, choose a time to present yours in private so your siblings won't feel diminished.

FATHER'S DAY

In most countries that observe Father's Day, it's celebrated on the third Sunday in June. In other countries, the first or second Sunday in September or the second Sunday in November is popular. Whatever the date, it's a holiday to honor Dad's contribution to the family.

What to write in your letter. Say you're thinking of him with fondness on this special day. Describe treasured memories that demonstrate his warmth, love, and dedication to his family.

If you're writing to your husband or partner, say what you appreciated about him early in your relationship and also what you especially like today about his parenting. Tell about his values you admire and his positive examples for your own behavior and that of your children. End your letter by expressing hope for a long life together while professing your love and devotion.

If you're writing to your father, tell him what you always appreciated about him when you were a child, and what you especially appreciate about him today. You may want to mention memories that demonstrate hard lessons he had to teach you. Tell about the values you've learned from him— ones you've already adopted or plan to adopt. Describe how your relationship has matured as you have grown, explaining what it's like today. You can find more ideas on what to write under Ideas for Writing to Your Parents, later in this chapter. End your letter by thanking him for the love and support he has always shown you; then express your own ongoing love for him.

How to present your letter. Ideas for framing or presenting your letter abound in the Part 1 chapter Present It. Try to present it in person. If you have siblings who don't have letters of their own to present, choose a time to present yours in private so your siblings won't feel diminished.

GRANDPARENTS DAY

For the countries that observe Grandparents Day, this holiday was established in the latter half of the 20th century. In the U.S., National Grandparents Day is celebrated in September on the first Sunday after Labor Day. In some other countries, Grandparents Day takes place in January, March, or October.

While the holiday is not yet as widely observed as Mother's Day or Father's Day, its purpose is to give children the chance to show their love and appreciation to their grandparents—and it gives grandparents the opportunity to reciprocate. Often the holiday celebration is extended to honor older adults outside the family, including individuals who act as adoptive grandparents toward neighborhood children.

What to write in your letter. Convey that you're thinking of your grandparent with fondness on this special day. Describe some treasured memories that demonstrate your grandparent's warmth, love, and dedication to the children and grandchildren.

If you're writing to your grandparent, tell what you always appreciated about him or her when you were a child, and what you especially appreciate today. You may want to mention treasured memories of fun things you did together. Describe the values you learned from him or her that you have already adopted or that you plan to adopt in your life. Explain how your relationship has matured as you've grown, and what it's like today. End your letter by thanking your grandparent for the love and support always shown to you and your family, and then express your own ongoing love.

If you're writing to a neighborhood grandparent figure, mention what you have always appreciated about him or her. You may want to mention treasured memories about fun things you did together—baking, fishing, gardening, working puzzles, or playing games, for example. Describe the values you've learned from him or her that you've already adopted or that you plan to adopt. Describe what your relationship is like today. End your letter by thanking your grandparent figure for the affection he or she has always shown you and your family and perhaps your neighborhood friends, and then express your fondness.

If you're a parent writing to your own mother or father, say what you've always appreciated about your grandparent when you were a child—and what you especially appreciate today. You may want to mention memories that demonstrate hard lessons he or she had to teach you. Describe the values you've learned from him or her that you have adopted in your life and passed along to the grandchildren. Describe how your relationship has matured as you have become an adult and a parent yourself. Say what parenthood is like for you today.

Describe what you treasure about how he or she treats your children. Ideas for Writing to Your Parents, which follows, contains more ideas on what to write. End your letter by thanking your parent for the love and support always shown to you and your children, and then express your own ongoing love for him or her.

How to present your letter. Ideas for framing or presenting your letter abound in the Part 1 chapter Present It. Try to present it in person. If you have siblings who don't have letters of their own to present, choose a time to present yours in private so your siblings won't feel diminished.

IDEAS FOR WRITING TO YOUR PARENTS

This section features wonderful ideas on what to include when you're writing to your parents—whether the occasion is your own engagement or marriage, Mother's Day, Father's Day, Grandparents Day, your parents' milestone wedding anniversary, or a milestone birthday celebration for one of your parents.

Consider the parenting techniques they demonstrated. Did your parents use tough love or gentle persuasion? Did they make you a partner in their decisions or discipline? Were they quietly firm, confident, understanding? Did they use a system of rewards and consequences? Did they engage in humor and/or gross exaggeration to make their points? Did they put a strong emphasis on education? Write about how their main parenting techniques benefited you growing up.

Mention specific treasured memories, if space permits.
These questions may spark some memories for you:

> Was one family vacation especially memorable?
> In what way? Describe it. If your parents had a
> family business, were you involved? If so, what did
> that experience teach you? What leisure activities—
> picnics, camping, boating, reading, golfing, bike
> riding, plays/musicals, games, sports, amusement
> parks—brought you closer together as a family?
> What made these experiences special to you? Did you
> take Sunday drives or long road trips together as a
> family? What were those like? What kind of positive
> memories do you have about those road trips? Did
> you sing songs or play instruments together? Does a
> particular song bring to mind a funny, joyful, or
> loving situation between you and your parents?

> Was one parent an exceptionally great cook?
> What stands out in your home cooking or dining
> experience? Did you and a parent ever build or cook
> something together? How did that go? Were you and
> either parent involved in any sports activities together?
> Did a particular disciplinary action from your parents
> make you a better person today? What one-to-one
> shared times or events did you enjoy together? For
> example, you may recall learning to read while
> enjoying books or the Sunday comics together,
> camping, playing catch, building a go-cart, playing
> checkers, even "getting to win" a favorite card game.

What emphasis was placed on education while you were growing up? Did your parents insist you get good grades and go to college? Did they help you with your homework? Did they volunteer in school activities?

If you're writing a letter to commemorate your parents' milestone wedding anniversary, do you have any special memories of the two of them behaving in a cute or romantic way? Were they particularly considerate toward one another in their day-to-day dealings? Did you hear and remember any inside jokes they enjoyed with each other? What are some reasons you think their marriage has lasted this long? Be candid.

Describe the important life lessons your parents taught you. Examples could include boundaries, friendship, integrity, generosity, moral standards, or appropriate behaviors. If you're getting married, how will the future for you and your spouse improve because of what you have learned? *Make this the strongest part of your letter.*

If you're writing to parents with special circumstances, read the following suggestions to spark your thinking about what to mention in your letter. Remember to express *your* feelings on these matters—be kind, positive, and truthful.

> *Parents who adopted you in infancy:* Write your letter as heartfelt as if they were your birth parents. You may want to say how grateful you feel to have been chosen to be a member of the family.

> *Parents who adopted you later in your childhood:* Acknowledge that their decision to adopt an older child may not have been an easy one. Write that you are honored to have been accepted as part of the family and that you hope you have made them proud.

> *Parent who adopted you after marrying your birth parent:* In the adoptive parent's paragraph, express gratitude

for the decision to welcome you into the family as his or her own child.

Birth parents who are divorced or separated: Write a separate letter for each parent. In these letters, you may choose (but need not feel obligated) to mention the other parent in the context of a treasured memory, for example.

Birth parents who have remarried: Write a separate letter for each birth parent. In these letters, you may choose (but need not feel obligated) to mention the other birth parent in the context of a treasured memory, for example.

Stepparents: You may want to honor a stepparent with an individual letter, especially if the remarriage took place before you left home. In it, you can acknowledge positive parenting and perhaps express your gratitude for being treated as if you were that stepparent's natural child.

Single parent: If you've always had just one parent, you might write about how your birth parent did such a good job that you never desired a second parent. You could also mention how this created a special relationship between the two of you.

Parent who was widowed before you left home: Discuss how much you appreciated having wonderful parents, and add fond memories that involve both parents. Then acknowledge that even though the two of you went through tough times when the other parent died, you appreciate that your surviving parent still did his or her best to pick up the pieces and continue to be a good parent to you.

Parent who was widowed after you left home: Tell how much you appreciate having had two wonderful parents while you were growing up. Bring up fond memories that involve both of them.

Another relative who raised you: Acknowledge his or her positive parenting attributes, and express gratitude for being accepted into the household as if you were that relative's own child. Write that you are honored to have been accepted into the family and hope you have made him or her proud.

IDEAS FOR WRITING TO YOUR SON OR DAUGHTER

Within this section, you'll find wonderful ideas on what to include when writing to your son or daughter—whether the occasion is your child's own milestone birthday, school- or career-related celebration, or engagement or marriage.

Mention specific treasured memories, if space permits. These questions may spark some memories for you: Did either of you build or cook something with your child, or was either of you involved with your child in such activities as sports or music? How did that go? If you had a family business, was your child involved? If so, what did that teach him or her? What leisure activities—picnics, camping, boating, reading, golfing, bike riding, plays/musicals, games, sports, amusement parks, Sunday drives or longer road trips, or singing or playing instruments together—brought you closer together as a family? What made these experiences special?

What one-to-one shared times or events did you enjoy together? For example, you may recall teaching your child to read books or the Sunday comics, camping, playing catch, building a go-cart, or playing checkers or a favorite card game and "letting" him or her win. Was one holiday celebration especially memorable? Which one, and what made it special?

What emphasis was placed on education while your child was growing up? Did you insist on good grades and going to college? Did you help with homework? Did you volunteer in school activities? Do you want to allude to any secrets, inside jokes, or special sayings that you share with your child? Did you have any good laughs or cries together?

If you're writing to your son or daughter with special circumstances, here are some specific suggestions to spark your thinking about what you would like to write; remember to express *your* feelings on these matters—be kind, positive, and truthful.

Child adopted in infancy: Write your letter as heartfelt as if you were your child's birth parents. You may want to say briefly how grateful you are to have him or her as a member of your family.

Child adopted later in his or her childhood: Acknowledge that your child's joining the family may have required some adjustment on his or her part. Write that you are honored to have been accepted as adoptive parents, and that he or she has made you proud.

Child whom one of you adopted after marrying the child's birth parent: Individually or in one section of a joint letter, the adoptive parent can express gratitude for the opportunity to be part of the adoptive child's life.

Child whose birth parents are separated, divorced, or remarried: Each birth parent can write a separate letter to your child. In these letters, you may each choose (but need not feel obligated) to mention the other parent in the context of a treasured memory or shared event, for example.

Stepchild: You can honor a stepchild with an individual letter, especially if your own marriage took place before your stepchild left home. In it, you can acknowledge positive parenting experiences and perhaps express gratitude for being treated as wonderfully as if you had been his or her birth parent.

Child of a single parent: If you raised your child alone, you might write about the special relationship this circumstance created between the two of you.

Child who, before leaving home, lost one parent: Mention fond family memories that include your child and both parents. Then acknowledge that even though you and your child went through tough times after the other parent died, you appreciate that your child did a good job picking up the pieces and continuing to be loving and supportive toward you.

Child who, after leaving home, lost one parent: Tell how much you appreciated family life while your child was growing up. Mention fond family memories that include your child and both parents.

Child who was raised by another relative (you): Express gratitude for being accepted in a parental role and describe what a pleasure it has been to raise him or her.

Child entering an arranged marriage: Express confidence that the new marriage will be successful; it involves two wonderful people pledging their full commitment to each other and their future together.

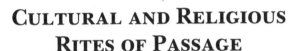

CULTURAL AND RELIGIOUS RITES OF PASSAGE

Faith is a knowledge within the heart,
beyond the reach of proof.

—Kahlil Gibran

Cultural traditions and religious faiths worldwide include a variety of initiation rites. Several popular examples have been included in this chapter, but it's by no means an all-inclusive list. If you don't see the specific cultural or religious practice that relates to the letter you plan to write—or if you'd like more information—consult an authority in your local religious or cultural community. You might also check with family and friends of the honoree, because many people's customs vary from traditional ways.

In addition, quietly contemplate the true meaning of the occasion as it relates to the person you plan to write to. If you still lack sufficient information, express your sincere congratulations and your best wishes.

BIRTH

Most world religions and cultures have a religious rite or sacrament relating to the birth of a child. Examples are a Catholic or Protestant baptism, a naming ceremony such as the Hindu *namakarana*, a circumcision and naming such as the Judaic *b'rit milah*, or *bris*, and more. In all cases, the rite welcomes the child to the religious community and affirms a commitment to the child's welfare through the godparents or the larger religious community.

Examples of birth rites. Rites that take place *at birth*, such as the Islamic rite of whispering the words of *adhan* (call to the prayer) in the newborn's right ear; *at 7 days old*, such as the Islamic naming ceremony for a new baby, or announcing a Jewish female baby's name at synagogue; *at 8 days old*, such as the Judaic covenant of male circumcision or the naming ritual among some West African indigenous cultures; or *at 1 month old*, such as a Chinese banquet celebrating the birth of the child and announcing its gender on the invitations. ("Happiness in playing with tiles" means it's a girl, and "Happiness in playing with jade" means it's a boy.)

When a baby gets older, other rites come into play. *At 3 to 6 months old*, a Catholic baby undergoes baptism, the first sacrament of initiation, which includes a blessing by the priest and a promise on the part of the congregation and the godparents to help support and provide for the child's Christian upbringing. In the Hindu faith, the rites of *annaprashana* (the offering of solid food to the child for the first time) and *chudakarna* (the child's first haircut) are observed.

What to write in your letter. All such ceremonies can be reason for a close relative or family member to write a letter to the parents or even to the child. It then becomes a treasured memento to be saved always. In the letter, you can express hope for the family's joy and prosperity together, and also for the baby's future as an individual who will bring joy to the family and someday bring honor to the broader community.

How to present your letter. You may choose to mail your letter or present it personally at a time you consider most appropriate. Take into consideration the type of occasion, the custom, and whether you live close to the recipient.

CHILDHOOD

As children grow, they become more fully integrated into the traditions of their family's religion or community's culture. Some initiation rites or customs observed in childhood can inspire writing a letter of congratulations to the child.

Examples of childhood initiation rites. The second sacrament of initiation in the Catholic faith is confirmation, considered the "perfection of baptism," which was the first sacrament of initiation. This second sacrament is received "in due time." This can mean at the time of baptism or as part of the child's religious education during grade school or even high school.

In Islam, a boy's circumcision ritual may take place anytime *between 8 days and 10 years of age,* representing a covenant between God and human beings.

At about age 12, Catholic children who have already received confirmation undergo the sacrament of the Holy Communion, or First Communion. This rite represents the first time children partake of one of the central practices of the Catholic faith, the Holy Eucharist, without which it is believed a Catholic would have difficulty resisting sin and temptation. Children prepare for their First Communion with two years of religious education, or catechism, at a local church. On the day of the rite, usually a celebration after church for family and friends is planned. The children are given gifts, such as a Bible, crucifix, gift basket, or prayer cards.

In Japanese Shintoism, November 3 is celebrated as *Shichi-Go-San* (literally translated as "seven-five-three"). On this day, *girls age seven and three and boys age five* don formal attire and come to the shrine where they petition the *kami* (powerful deities) for health and prosperity.

In Hinduism, the *upanayana,* or sacred-thread ceremony, marks initiation into studentship, such as the introduction of Hindu boys (and sometimes girls) to a Vedic guru, a spiritual teacher of the Vedas (Hindu sacred writings). The word *upanayana* means "sitting close by," and the ceremony is considered a second birth. Sometimes the child receives a spiritual name from the priest or guru. The child takes vows to study the Vedas, serve the teachers, and follow certain vows, including celibacy. The ceremony often concludes with the child's offering the traditional *dakshina* (gift) to his or her teacher.

In Sikhism, the *amrit* is the baptism or ceremony of rebirth. Initiates can be males or females of any age, as long as they consider themselves ready to agree to worship one God, read the Guru Granth Sahib (the respected scripture of the supreme enlightener), join the Sikh congregation, serve others, and refrain from worshiping any created object or living thing.

These Sikhs must comply with a specific dress code for undergoing the rite. They must also vow not to cut their hair, smoke, or drink alcohol. For the remainder of their lives, they are obligated to keep the five Ks: *kesh* (their hair), *kara* (a steel bracelet to remind them to do good deeds for God), *kirpan* (a small sword with which to stand up for what is right), *kacchere* (shorts worn under the clothing to show goodness and action), and *kanga* (a small wooden comb carried as a sign of cleanliness).

What to write in your letter. Start with an expression of your congratulations, of course, on the honoree's having reached this milestone. Express pride in his or her accomplishment and a hope that this day marks the beginning of a future filled with joy and blessings.

From there, depending on the nature and significance of the rite, you could comment on the significance of the rite in the child's life. You can express hope that the experience may bless, guide, and inspire the child in all the days and years to come. You can also express confidence that the person will become an admirable young man or woman who religiously follows the spiritual values of the family or community. You can say that today's experience will cause the child to grow in faith, thus enriching his or her life and fulfilling the child's dreams. If appropriate, you could allude to following in the footsteps of faith that his or her parents, grandparents, and ancestors did.

In closing, you could offer best wishes for remaining true to the teachings and beliefs of the child's religious community. Also express your wishes for success in all he or she strives to achieve and for enjoying a future blessed with joy, prosperity, adventure, friendship, and a long and healthy life.

How to present your letter. You may choose to mail your letter or present it personally at a time you consider most appropriate. Take into consideration the type of occasion, the custom, and whether you live close to the recipient.

PUBERTY

Coming-of-age initiation rites are commonly observed in many religious faiths. The purpose is to strengthen the bond between the individual and his or her faith or religious community. At least some of these occasions might be considered appropriate for a parent or other close relative to write a letter to the child.

This section offers a brief overview of common rites for younger to older children among the major world religions. Following this overview are suggestions for what to include in such a letter.

Examples of initiation rites. In the Theravada Buddhist tradition in Southeast Asia, coming of age takes place for boys and some girls *between the ages of 8 and 12 years*, when they are initiated into adulthood to become a novice monk or nun. To begin with, they are dressed as princes and princesses like Prince Gautama. They accept the Three Jewels or cornerstones—Buddha, the teacher; dharma, the teachings or laws; and *sangha*, the community of believers—after which their heads are shaved and they change into saffron robes. The children may then stay with the monks from one night to a few years.

In Judaism, on the Sabbath following a boy's *13th birthday* or following a girl's *12th or 13th birthday* (for Orthodox or Reform/ Liberal communities, respectively), the child is considered old enough to assume religious duties and therefore becomes an adult in the eyes of the religious community. The boys' initiation rite is called a *bar mitzvah* (meaning "son of the commandment"); the girls' initiation rite is called a *bat mitzvah* (meaning "daughter of the commandment"). During the ceremony, the boy or girl reads in Hebrew from the Torah scroll.

In Central Africa, the rite of transforming a boy or girl into an adult involves a period of separation from the community, which for males usually also involves circumcision. This is followed by a return to the community, but in seclusion, where they are treated as a non-person but taught how to behave as an adult while being trained in traditional gender roles and adult skills. Finally, the individuals are integrated back into the community during a coming-out ritual, for which occasion they wear new clothes as they are accepted into adulthood.

In West African indigenous cultures, which often also observe Christianity or Islam, the cultural rite of transforming into an adult involves segregation from the community and from the opposite sex, shaving of heads to symbolize new life after the ritual, fasting, silence, male circumcision (if this was not already done in infancy due to the influence of Christianity or Islam) and sometimes female circumcision, and sometimes, for males, a ritual death consisting of food deprivation and sleep deprivation.

In Japanese Shintoism, January 15 is Coming of Age Day, known as *Seijin-Shiki* or *Seijin-no-Hi*. On this day, all *20 year olds* celebrate officially becoming part of the adult community by wearing special garb and visiting a Shinto shrine with their friends. After that, they go to a city rally to hear speeches by government officials; and after that, they often go out to dinner with friends and family.

What to write in your letter. Start with an expression of your congratulations, of course, on having reached this milestone. Express pride in the young person's accomplishment and a hope that this day will begin a future filled with joy and blessings.

From there, depending on the nature and significance of the rite, you could comment on the significance of the rite in the honoree's life; express confidence that the person will become an admirable young man or woman who religiously follows the family or community's spiritual values; express hope that the experience will bless, guide, and inspire the honoree every day of his or her adult life, and that the young person will be inspired to become a responsible adult worthy of emulation by siblings and others and a source of joy to family and friends. If appropriate, you could allude to following, in faith, in the footsteps of his or her parents, grandparents, and ancestors.

In closing, you could offer best wishes for remaining true to the teachings and beliefs of the religious community; for success in all he or she strives to achieve; and for a future blessed with joy, prosperity, adventure, friendship, and a long and healthy life.

How to present your letter. You may choose to mail your letter or present it personally at a time you consider most appropriate, taking into consideration the type of occasion, the custom, and whether you are local to the recipient.

MARRIAGE

The rite of marriage is observed and revered in every faith and culture. It's probably the most joyful reason to write a letter of appreciation. However, these letters typically focus more on the non-religious significance of the occasion than on the rite itself. So for detailed writing suggestions, read the information provide under the following sections:

- ◆ Marriage (in the Romance chapter)
- ◆ Ideas for Writing a Romantic Letter (in the Romance chapter)
- ◆ Ideas for Writing to Your Parents (in the Family chapter)
- ◆ Ideas for Writing to Your Son or Daughter (in the Family chapter)

DEATH

Every religion or culture shows respect when someone from within their community dies. Funerals or memorial services in Western cultures, Hindu *antyesthi* (cremation), Islamic burial ritual, and the Central African ritual of transforming a newly deceased person's spirit into a good ancestor make up a few examples of how this respect is demonstrated.

You may be asked to deliver a eulogy at the funeral or memorial service. Or you may wish to prepare other remarks that you or someone else will read at the service. Or you may want to observe the passing of your friend or loved one by writing something more personal or private.

The purpose and content of your letter. Is the purpose of your letter to show others how much this person meant to you? Or is it to express your private thoughts to the deceased because you never had the opportunity or could never muster the courage to voice those thoughts when he or she was alive? Are these thoughts loving and kind, or do they express something very personal regarding the deceased that you need to "get off your chest"? All of these are valid reasons to write. In many cases, the writing furthers the grieving process or helps provide closure.

For guidance on what to write, refer to the information under Eulogies and Public Tributes and perhaps also Personal Letters to Deceased Friends and Loved Ones, in the Part 3 chapter Bringing Meaning to a Life Well Lived.

How to present your letter. You may read a eulogy or other public tribute aloud in the memorial or funeral service. Or you may read your personal letter silently or aloud in private at a later time at the graveside, at a shrine or temple, beside a fountain, or in a beautiful garden or natural setting with running water. You may even read it in the privacy of your home by candlelight, perhaps with soothing music or running water from a fountain in the background.

The contents and purpose of your writing will help you determine what to do with your letter after you have presented or read it. Perhaps you will save the letter in a special location, burn it, shred it by hand and toss it into the wind, attach it to a balloon and release it into the sky, or even place it in an envelope with flowers at graveside. If what you wrote was positive, you might even wish to give it to the family of the deceased. That way, they will know your thoughts and feelings about their loved one.

ANCESTRAL RITES

A number of religions worldwide hold special rites or celebrations to honor their deceased ancestors. If you knew and treasured any ancestors when they were living, consider writing a letter to them individually. You can then ceremoniously read your letter and perhaps burn it afterwards or save it for your descendants to help them know their ancestors better.

Examples of ancestral rites. In Japanese Shintoism, March 22 is *Mitama-Matsuri,* the Festival for the Ancestral Spirits, to acknowledge people and families who helped sustain the institution of the shrine. In Hinduism, the *pitra-tarpan* is observed for two weeks in September/October each year to honor one's deceased parents, grandparents, and ancestors.

The Latin American culture celebrates *El Día de los Muertos,* or Day of the Dead. It is usually observed in the first two days of November, but it lasts an entire week in Mexico. During *El Día de los Muertos,* the message conveys that death is not the end of life but rather the renewal of life, a ritual that promises rebirth.

In Mexico, November 1 is *Día de Todos los Santos* (All Saints Day), which honors all Christian saints and martyrs, and November 2 begins the official celebration of the dead, a time of family reunion for the living as well as the dead. The spirit of this celebration in Mexico is based on a belief that the dead deserve a vacation, too, so they return to earth once a year for family fun. The celebration includes decorated cemeteries, musicians, and even masked dancers in front of the church.

In one region of Guatemala, boys fly large colorful kites over the cemetery. In a village in Peru, offerings of food are blessed by the priest and left for the dead in cemeteries.

In Central Africa, ancestors are honored through rituals and also asked to ward off danger, tensions, and other problems in the family or community. Often, ancestral spirits are honored within the home, with the eldest man or woman in the home saying prayers and offering objects. In West Africa, the remembered dead are seen as intermediaries between the living world and the dead world. Favorite foods and/or tokens of esteem are placed near their graves to honor them.

What to write in your letter. If you have memories of the ancestors you wish to honor with a letter, you may either write to them directly or address your letter to their living descendants as you tell about their ancestors. For example, you can write a joint letter to your deceased grandmother and grandfather; you can write individual letters to each of them; or you can write to your parents or your children about your beloved grandparents.

In the letters, you can describe their positive qualities, your recollections of treasured experiences or "grand adventures" you shared together, and the values you learned from them that make you a better person today. Find more information about what to write under Personal Letters to Deceased Friends and Loved Ones in the Part 3 chapter Bringing Meaning to a Life Well Lived.

How to present your letter. If your letter is written to your ancestors directly, then you may choose to read it aloud during a ceremony (if permitted) or else read it (silently or aloud) in private at a later time at the graveside, at a shrine or temple, beside a fountain, or in a beautiful garden or natural setting. You can even read it in the privacy of your home by candlelight, perhaps with soothing music (or your ancestor's favorite music) playing in the background.

The contents and purpose of such a letter will help you determine what to do with it after reading it. Perhaps you will save it in a special place, ceremonially burn it, shred it by hand and toss it into the wind, or attach it to a balloon and release it into the sky. You can even place it in an envelope with flowers at graveside. You might also wish to give your letter (or a copy of it) to your children, so they will know their ancestors better.

PROFESSION OF FAITH, RELIGIOUS CONSECRATION, AND ORDINATION

Regardless of the type of ordination or religious advancement, it is appropriate to honor the individual who has chosen to make a formal commitment to serve his or her faith in an official role, even if you do not happen to be of the same faith as the person being ordained.

Examples of ordination rites. The Buddhist community consists of monks, nuns, laymen, and laywomen. For Buddhists worldwide, the most fundamental ritual for both monastic and lay Buddhists is *to take refuge.* This marks the practitioner's entry, or initiation, into the Buddhist tradition. The refuge ceremony is performed in which the initiate recites three times, "I take refuge in the Buddha [meaning the community of all buddhas], dharma, and *sangha,*" which affirms the practitioner's commitment in body, speech, and mind. (This is also known as the Three Jewels). Thereafter, they adhere to the precepts of right ethics, meditative cultivation, and cultivation of wisdom.

Ritual ordination for Buddhist monks and nuns takes place in two stages: initially as a novice and later as a fully ordained *bhikshu* (almsman), a nun, or (in a minority of Buddhist countries), a *bhikshuni* (almswoman). The ritual of ordination involves head shaving, monastic robes, and an alms bowl, plus adopting a new ordination name, usually taking a vow of celibacy, and thereafter refraining from intoxicants and certain entertainments.

In the Roman Catholic faith, married or unmarried men can be ordained as deacons assisting priests and bishops. Some unmarried deacons who have additional training can be ordained as priests and be considered co-workers of the bishops. And some priests can be ordained as bishops who, as a body, are considered the successors of the Apostles. Finally, from among the ranks of bishops, some of whom have been elevated to the office of cardinal, a pope is selected by the College of Cardinals to serve as the Bishop of Rome and Saint Peter's successor, head of the Catholic Church.

Some men and women in the Catholic Church are called to religious life through another path. The initial period of spiritual training is the novitiate, and the individuals are called novices during this three-stage process. The first stage lasts one to two years, during which participants are called postulants. Then the individuals are officially accepted and enter the second stage, spending another one to two years in spiritual formation.

The final stage of the novitiate lasts three to five years. It begins with their taking temporary vows. After they do, they can be called brothers or sisters as they spend those years working or continuing their theological education or regular degreed programs. At the end of the novitiate, brothers and sisters take final, permanent vows. Note that monks and nuns are brothers and sisters who have chosen a vocation that is "restricted by enclosure," such as living in a monastery or convent.

The various branches of the protestant and Latter Day Saints faiths have their own religious hierarchies, sometimes involving a combination of deacons, religious practitioners, lay or Stephen ministers, Melchizedek and Aaronic priests, assistant ministers, ministers, vicars, rectors, priests, bishops, archbishops, and other comparable titles.

In Judaism, there is no hierarchy. The rabbi (a religious teacher and person authorized to make decisions based on Jewish law) and chazzan or cantor (a person who leads the congregation in prayer) are each hired by the synagogue's board of directors. A rabbi's training generally involves initial testing: Usually but not always rabbis attend college for at least four years; then they spend five to six years (including possible internships) in seminary or yeshiva. Optionally, they spend a year in Israel to develop a relationship with Israel and a familiarity with Hebrew as a living language. Finally, they complete graduation or ordination, which involves diplomas or certifications.

In polytheistic tribes of West Africa, there is no formal hierarchy of priests. Instead, a community or tribe is overseen by either tribal elders or shamans (priests and priestesses). Sometimes a shaman comes from the same lineage as the previous shaman; other times, a shamanic initiation may result when a spirit guide has come to a young individual through many dreams. Sometimes, a potential future shaman may be seen in someone who has cured himself or herself, purportedly with the help of a spirit who has come in guidance.

What to write in your letter. Because appropriate forms of address on the envelope and in your letter's salutation will vary from one faith to the next, check with your local religious or spiritual authority or perhaps search the Internet for guidance. For example, a Catholic priest named John Smith would be indicated on the envelope as "Rev. Smith" (note the abbreviation); a formal salutation would read "Dear Reverend Father" (with no first or last name), and an informal salutation would read "Dear Father Smith." A Catholic sister named Mary Jones would be indicated on the envelope as "Sister Mary Jones," a formal salutation would read "Dear Sister Mary Jones," and an informal salutation would read "Dear Sister Mary."

It is appropriate to begin your letter with congratulations, of course; then:

> *If you're a member of the congregation or community the honoree is leaving* as a result of ordination, you may tell about the religious experiences you have shared together and the positive example the person has set within the religious community. Then you can wish him or her well in the new role and religious duties, and end with an appropriate complimentary close, such as "Go with God" or "May Buddha guide you."

> *If you're a family member,* after your congratulations you can include more personal memories of how you have observed the individual's development within the community of the faithful. You can describe this person's positive traits that you believe will serve him or her well in the new religious role being assumed, and then end with a more familiar, yet still religiously appropriate complimentary close, such as "Go with God and our love" or "May your guiding spirit and our love protect you."

> *If you're a friend,* start your letter by offering your congratulations. If you are of the same religious persuasion, you can include personal memories of how you have observed the individual's development within the community of the faithful. Regardless of whether you share the same faith, you can still describe this person's positive traits that you believe will serve him or her well in the new religious role being assumed. End with a friendly yet still religiously appropriate complimentary close, such as "I will keep you in fond memory as you go with God" or "May God and all the saints protect you, and may you know the support of our friendship in the years ahead."

How to present your letter. Deliver your letter personally, if you can. If you'll be bringing it to a formal event that should not be interrupted, your letter can be folded and placed in a sealed envelope for later reading. If an informal celebration is scheduled later on, you might deliver it personally in an unsealed envelope. If distance or circumstances prevent a personal delivery, mail your letter instead.

The author wishes to acknowledge the following resource, which provided background for the rites and rituals described in this chapter for Islam, Judaism, Shintoism, Hinduism, and Buddhism, as well as for the cultures of Latin America, West Africa, and Central Africa: Frank A. Salamone (Ed.), *The Routledge Encyclopedia of Religious Rites, Rituals, and Festivals* (New York and London: Routledge, 2004).

CAREER

*A group becomes a team when each member is sure
enough of himself and his contribution
to praise the skills of others.*

—Norman Shidle

When you tell people at work you appreciate their efforts, chances are they feel good, they keep doing their best, and their positive attitude spreads to those around them. But the words are soon forgotten, so the effect is short term. On the other hand, when you take the time to *write* to your supervisor, co-worker, or employee to express your appreciation, your letter has more "staying power" than spoken words because it can be re-experienced every time it's read. The benefits are great and potentially far reaching; for example, enhanced personal motivation, increased job satisfaction, and a more positive and productive overall working environment. Yes, this pleasurable investment of time yields great dividends for worker and company alike.

ABOVE-AND-BEYOND EFFORTS: SPECIAL PROJECTS

Employees make special efforts all the time to meet deadlines, launch new products, help make a big promotion a smashing success, and more. If they receive any recognition at all, it's usually just a pat on the back or a public or private "Good job!" from the supervisor, perhaps when passing in the hall. Those recognitions are beneficial, as far as they go.

But imagine the longer-lasting impact of a personal letter of appreciation describing why you value them.

On the other side of the coin, an employee or a group of employees might want to appreciate an immediate supervisor or even the president of the company. The recipient may have "gone the extra mile" on behalf of the employees or helped the employees make a success of the company as a whole—which benefits employees in terms of job security. Or employees may appreciate a leader's role in a special situation, such as a product launch. Granted, it's unusual for employees to honor a supervisor or company leader with a letter of appreciation for such efforts—but for that reason, it will be all the more special to the recipient.

If you're a supervisor writing to your team of employees, each employee will appreciate a personalized letter. Using mail-merge capability, create letters with a personalized address block, salutation line, and employee name to begin the final paragraph. Remember to include "cc: Human Resources" at the bottom of the letter, and follow through by providing your HR department with a duplicate copy of each letter to add to each employee's official personnel file.

Start your letter by acknowledging the successful outcome of the product launch, promotional campaign, or other accomplishment. You can cite facts, figures, and others' feedback to support your assessment, and be sure to note it was a team effort. If *every* team member was part of that successful outcome, then specifically cite the individual contributions of each team member. Or, you can name all the employees within a given task group and note the achievements of the group. However, if not every team member made a special effort, maintain your integrity by writing generally about the accomplishments of all the smaller task groups, without stating employees' names. Then start your final paragraph with the employee's name and restate your appreciation.

At a team meeting, thank everyone as a group for helping, distribute the individual letters to each person present, and then wrap up by repeating your appreciation.

If you're a supervisor writing to an individual employee, start by acknowledging the successful outcome of the product launch, promotional campaign, or other accomplishment. You can cite facts, figures, and others' feedback to support your assessment. Then mention the key role your employee played in the positive outcome. Be specific. Close by thanking the employee for his or her efforts in this launch, campaign, or other activity (which you'll describe briefly), and note that he or she is an asset to the department and the company.

Because others in the department aren't necessarily receiving a letter of their own, it's best to present this letter privately. Depending on your personal management style, you may choose to read your letter aloud to your employee at that time, or briefly state your appreciation and hand the letter to your employee in a sealed or unsealed envelope. Again, make sure Human Resources receives a copy of this letter to place in the employee's personnel file.

If you're an employee writing to your supervisor, make sure it's to express appreciation for actions or behavior consistent with company policy—not for something like granting you undocumented personal time off. Your supervisor will appreciate knowing you gave a copy of this letter to his or her boss and to Human Resources for inclusion in his or her personnel file. (Indicate this at the bottom of your letter below your signature block. Type "cc:" and then, on the first line, provide the full name, title, and department of your supervisor's boss and, on the second line, "Human Resources.")

Start your letter by saying you realize it's unusual for employees to write letters of this kind to their supervisors.

Then explain you were inspired to write because you appreciate his or her recent actions (or ongoing behavior) as your supervisor. If you're writing about your supervisor's particular actions on behalf of the employees or a company or departmental goal, explain what impressed you in particular and why you're grateful. If the letter describes ongoing behavior you admire, again explain why you're impressed and grateful. Close your letter with how privileged you are to be working for someone who's such a good influence on you and your department and who means so much to the company as a whole.

You may send or deliver this letter in a large sealed envelope addressed to your supervisor, optionally marking it "Personal and Confidential—Please Deliver Unopened."

If you're an employee (or group of employees) writing to someone in upper management, your letter will be a bit more formal but still reflect your own writing style. Perhaps your letter is inspired by something this individual did or said on behalf of the company or employees, such as a positive interview on TV, or a quotation or article in online news or the newspaper. Or maybe it relates to something this manager did to advocate for the employees as a whole or for your department. Or perhaps you've observed over time how ethical and hard working this person is. Whatever the case, express your heartfelt appreciation in your letter.

Start by saying what inspired you to write, in general. Then be more specific regarding this individual's behavior or actions. You may want to describe how or why this person's actions or decisions stood out to you compared to routine management behavior. Be sure to focus on the positive instead of dwelling on other managers' negative behavior, if any. Rather, explain that the individual's actions or statements were or are more far reaching, caring, or involved than one might expect from someone in a managerial position. In closing, state what an honor it is to be working for a company with such fine leadership.

In the signature block, if one or only a few employees are sending the letter and space permits, leave room for all to sign, with their typewritten names appearing below where they sign. Otherwise, skip the typewritten names and instead use a typewritten generic term such as "The Team in Department 55" and have everyone sign in the blank space below. Then below the entire signature area, write "cc: Human Resources" and provide a duplicate to your Human Resources department with a request to include it in the manager's own personnel file. This letter can be presented to the manager personally by the writer(s) or their designated representative, or it can be sent in a large envelope addressed to that individual.

MILESTONE WORK ANNIVERSARY

In today's world of corporate and individual volatility, it can be unusual for an employee to remain with a company for even 5 years, much less 10, 15, or 20. Such occasions are worth commemorating—and not with just a service pin (although that's a classy touch). A more personal approach is a brief letter from the person's immediate supervisor or the head of the company (or both, as two separate letters). These letters can thank the employee for past service and acknowledge the employee's continuing commitment to the company.

If you're the employee's immediate supervisor, start your letter by thanking the employee for past service. Then describe a couple of his or her specific contributions in recent years that clearly demonstrate the person's unique value to the department and/or company. Close by declaring that the employee is a genuine asset and you hope both the company and employee will continue to benefit from the mutually productive relationship. You can present this letter—and perhaps read it aloud—at a team or department meeting.

If you're representing upper management, naturally you won't know as much about this employee's personal contribution as the immediate supervisor does. If the supervisor is writing a separate letter to commemorate the work anniversary, leave those specifics to him or her to describe. However, if yours is the only letter to be presented to the employee, then you can make your letter more memorable by taking time to talk to the supervisor. In your discussion, find out why this employee is well liked; then incorporate what the supervisor said in your letter.

Start your letter by congratulating the employee on having completed X years of service and thanking him or her for efforts made during that time.

Then, if appropriate, include what the employee's supervisor has said about him or her and comment that you're pleased to see the employee is so well thought of. If the supervisor is presenting a separate letter, instead of this, write how important it is to the company to retain such an experienced employee. In the final paragraph, express the hope of continuing this mutually beneficial working relationship for many years to come.

On this letter, too, copy both the supervisor and Human Resources so the letter of appreciation will be added to the employee's own file. If you don't personally present the letter, the employee's own supervisor can present it either privately or at a department meeting, and perhaps read it aloud.

BONUS OR AWARD

When an employee or group performs well on behalf of the company, the company may award a bonus based on resulting profitability and/or individual employee contributions toward successful company performance.

Smaller companies can emulate larger ones by announcing these bonuses via a mail-merge letter from the head of the company, with salutation and bonus details personalized. The first paragraph or two can describe the company's performance during the latest period (quarter, half, or full year) and thank the company team in general for helping to make that possible. The next paragraph recognizes each employee individually for his or her contribution toward that period's performance and provides details regarding the bonus (the amount as well as how and when it will be paid).

The following paragraph encourages everyone to continue to strive for high company achievement. It also emphasizes how important each employee's effort is toward continuing to achieve or exceed company goals within a challenging competitive environment.

The final paragraph again thanks the individual employee for his or her contributions to the company's success and ends with a "keep up the good work" type of statement.

Bonus letters are normally presented privately to the employee by the employee's immediate supervisor.

SALARY INCREASE

A company may award salary increases as a way to help employees keep up with inflation, as a union mandate, or as a reward for merit. When the increase is given as a reward, the good news is usually shared at the same time as the written performance appraisal. Sometimes it comes with a brief letter from the head of the company or division.

The first paragraph may indicate that the employee's supervisor recommended him or her for a salary increase based on contributions relative to that of peers within the company and perhaps within the industry overall. The letter then states the recommendation was supported and approved, and thanks the employee for his or her ongoing hard work to help the company in its efforts to be successful in the marketplace.

The details of the salary increase (e.g., job title, current weekly salary or hourly rate, amount of increase as a percent as well as dollar amount, new weekly salary or hourly rate, and effective date) may appear in the next paragraph or as an attachment. The next paragraph invites the employee to address any questions or concerns to his or her immediate supervisor, and the final paragraph thanks the employee once again for his or her efforts.

Salary-increase letters are normally presented to the employee privately by the employee's immediate supervisor.

PROMOTION

A promotion or change in job title may result when an employee exceeds expectations, shows promise of performing well in a new capacity, or qualifies for a higher pay level as a result of long-term experience on the job. All three circumstances call for a letter recognizing the employee's contributions. That letter is likely to come from the person authorizing the promotion.

If you're the employee's supervisor or person authorizing the promotion, your letter will begin by expressing congratulations on the promotion, mentioning the new job title, department (if different), and effective date. If the employee will remain in your department, state how much you're looking forward to the new working relationship. The next paragraph will list the increase in annual salary or hourly rate, as well as the new total weekly salary or hourly rate. In another paragraph, you can mention an attached job description (if any). If you will continue to be his or her supervisor, invite the employee to come to you with any questions or concerns. The final paragraph will repeat your congratulations and state that the promotion was well deserved. You'll no doubt be presenting your letter privately.

If you're the employee's spouse or significant other, give congratulations on the promotion, say it was well deserved, and express confidence he or she will exceed expectations in the new position. You may also describe how the promotion will affect the family's lifestyle. For example, if the promotion comes with a salary increase, describe how you believe the new salary may solve any of the family's recent or long-term financial difficulties or afford family members new financial or recreational opportunities.

If the working hours will move or increase, offer your support in making that transition a smooth one. If the new position involves more business travel, focus on the opportunity for him or her to enjoy new experiences but also on your readiness to assume added responsibilities during those absences. If the position involves less travel, focus on how pleasant it will be to enjoy his or her company more often. Tell about friendship, partnership, and achieving dreams together. Then close with best wishes for continued success. Your letter can be presented in person during a celebratory dinner or mailed, if more appropriate.

If you're a relative, personal friend, or work friend of the person being promoted, express your pleasure at hearing the news of the promotion. Then congratulate the employee on being promoted, indicate it was well deserved, and say you're confident that he or she will exceed expectations in the new position. Then close with best wishes for continued success.

Your letter can be presented in person during a celebratory lunch or mailed, if more appropriate.

RETIREMENT

In the mid and even late 20th century, a 65th birthday represented retirement for employees in the U.S. because that's when people could begin to collect the full amount of their Social Security income. These days, however, workers of Baby Boomer age and younger must wait until a later age before they can collect the full value of their Social Security retirement supplement. Also, for financial or other reasons, many people these days are working longer—sometimes well into their 70s and even beyond. To them, 65 is just another birthday, perhaps with a party—but then it's back to work!

When people eventually do choose to retire, it's a milestone event—a major transition into a new lifestyle. Retirees can begin to enjoy more activities with their spouse, adult children, grandchildren, and friends, which they simply couldn't do when working full time. Other times, people "retire" to pursue a new career, often involving self-employment in something they've always longed to do. Perhaps they will finally have time to engage in volunteer activities. On the other hand, retirement may be a case of need—to care for an ailing spouse or parent, or to watch grandchildren while both parents work to make ends meet. In any case, it's the beginning of a new phase of life.

At work, supervisors and co-workers aren't always aware of those special retirement circumstances, and it isn't always appropriate to ask the retiree a lot of questions, in case he or she desires privacy.

If you're the retiree's supervisor, the best approach is to write a letter of appreciation for the time and effort the employee has spent on the job. In such a letter, you can reflect on your first memories of that employee and describe how far the employee has come (at least, during your tenure). You can mention work challenges that the employee faced head-on and addressed effectively. It's appropriate to mention the employee's good work-related qualities and perhaps give an example or two of how the employee demonstrated the strongest of those qualities. If the employee is admired by co-workers within the department and perhaps by others outside, say so. And if the employee is well liked by customers or clients, mention that, too. In closing, restate the employee's value to the company, department, and you, and say he or she will be missed. And then wish the individual all the best for the future.

If the upcoming retirement is public knowledge, you can be courteous by letting others know the situation, in case they want to write their own letters of appreciation before the employee retires.

If you're the retiree's co-worker in the same department, discuss those positive qualities you've observed and perhaps benefited from firsthand, such as a helpful attitude or mentoring abilities. Or perhaps your co-worker was the go-to person for solving problems or knew where to send you for help. Say you'll miss the employee and wish him or her all the best in the future, inviting the person to stay in touch.

If you're a customer or other outside associate of the retiree, consider sending a duplicate copy of your farewell letter of appreciation to the retiree's immediate supervisor and perhaps to the Human Resources department for the employee's permanent file. (You never know; sometimes retirees decide to return, and your letter would be of benefit.)

If you're the husband, wife, son, or daughter of the retiree, write a personal letter expressing your congratulations and appreciation for all the years of dedication and hard work that benefited you and your family. Reflect on the security your family has enjoyed thanks to the retiree. Describe a couple of the leisure-time experiences (cruises, special vacations, etc.) you enjoyed together because of your family member's efforts at work. Express admiration for the hard-working dedication and motivation you've observed as your family member did what it took to ensure the family's security.

If you know your family member also enjoyed his or her career, say you're grateful he or she could find such joy and fulfillment at work.

If it applies, express gratitude for friendships and important contacts established by the retiree through work over the years, and describe how much these have meant to all of you.

Then refer to the future and how you'll be celebrating a lifestyle change with new opportunities, experiences, and adventures. Mention that he or she will now have the opportunity to pursue long-missed or long-desired hobbies and activities. Name a few of these, if you know them. (If you're the spouse, *don't* mention the honey-do list!)

And if you're the already-retired spouse, in an upbeat way, muse about the changes you both can expect in adjusting to your new roles. For example, you might playfully mention fighting over the TV remote or suggest cooking gourmet meals together.

In closing, say you're looking forward to these new adventures together and express your continuing love and support.

LETTER OF REFERENCE (RECOMMENDATION LETTER)

Letters of reference (LORs), also known as recommendation letters, are less common today than they once were because of concern about legal liability for a variety of issues, including discrimination. On the other hand, if an employee is laid off because the job has been eliminated or the plant has closed, the employer or supervisor could safely give the employee a letter clarifying this. The employee can duplicate and distribute the letter as appropriate when seeking new employment.

If you're the current or former supervisor of an employee or student intern who has asked you to write a recommendation letter, first be aware of the following. Unlike regular co-workers, supervisors are considered agents of their employer; so if supervisors engage in discriminatory behavior—even if unintended—they, as well as the employer, may be sued. Such lawsuits are not uncommon; and when they do occur, they cost the supervisor and the company both time and financial resources. Primarily to prevent these types of risks, most large companies and some smaller ones have established policies requiring their supervisors to refer all such LOR requests to their Human Resources department. Most likely, HR will then respond in writing only to the most direct written requests for verification of facts (such as name, job title, and salary), but not opinions (such as job performance). So before responding to a request for an LOR, consult your company policies first; then, if you do draft a letter, have HR review it to minimize legal exposure.

Even if your company allows its supervisors to write LORs, you're under no obligation to comply with a request to do so. If your workload is already too heavy, politely say that to the requesting employee. And if you can't *honestly* write anything positive in an LOR, don't write anything at all. Instead, say something like: "I may not be the best person to write this letter" or "I don't think it would be that helpful to you, but I wish you well."

Whether or not you perceive the employee to be an asset to the company, you might suggest to the employee that, in lieu of an LOR, prospective employers could be provided with photocopies of past positive performance appraisals.

If and when you do write an LOR, be as truthful as possible and use discretion in your choice of words. Stick to factual statements and avoid ambiguous words and phrases such as, "You'll never regret it if you hire this person." Yes, from a liability standpoint, you have limited legal protection when you tell the truth, but sometimes there's a fine line between truth and libel.

If the employee has signed a release with the prospective employer authorizing any previous employers to "disclose any information to the prospective employer," this relieves some of the dangers involved. However, you'll still want to use good judgment if you do divulge information.

If you're a co-worker (not the supervisor) of a regular employee or student intern who is requesting an LOR, you may have less liability than a supervisor would. That is, you may not be considered an agent of the company, and therefore the company would have some protection if your LOR proves problematic. However, because a co-worker's LOR carries less weight with a prospective employer than a supervisor's would, consider whether it's worth writing the letter at all.

If you're a teacher who supervised a student in a work-study program, LORs are more common in that situation. If you choose to write the LOR, first ask the student for a job description; then make sure the contents of your letter are relevant and sequenced conveniently for the prospective employer. Be factual and positive in your letter; e.g., "a diligent worker who always completes assigned tasks on schedule." Focus also on the character of the student worker—qualities that will continue to serve the individual well in the world of work. These might include, for example, reliability, capability, responsibility, dependability, respect, maturity, judgment, or generosity of spirit.

If you're a college professor of one of your current or former students applying to a graduate studies program, you might be asked to write an LOR as part of the application process. Note the following cautions before you commit to write such a letter:

◆ If you can't honestly write anything positive in an LOR, don't write anything at all. You can respond to the student by saying: "I may not be the best person to write this letter" or "I don't think it would be that helpful to you, but I wish you well." Not writing an LOR is better than writing a weak or unpleasantly honest one.

◆ If an LOR has been requested by one of your current students, first check to see if school policy permits this while you are still his or her teacher.

◆ Either way, you may also want to ask your dean or legal department if it's appropriate and permitted for you to write the letter. Also inquire about any possible discrimination-related pitfalls to bear in mind if you do write one.

Once you've agreed to write the LOR, ask the student for a written description of the graduate-program requirements. Then, make sure the contents of your letter are relevant and sequenced conveniently for the graduate studies screening authorities. Be factual and positive; e.g., "a particularly good student." Focus also on the character of the student—the qualities that would serve the student well in graduate studies, such as reliability, capability, responsibility, dependability, diligence, respect, maturity, judgment, or generosity of spirit. In your final paragraph, assess the student's capabilities in the context of your role as teacher; e.g., "Based on my work with this student, I (recommend/am confident/believe)...."

PART 3
WRITING FOR OCCASIONS MADE SPECIAL

HONORING TEACHERS, COACHES, MENTORS, AND STUDENTS

*Treat people as if they were what they should be,
and you help them become what they
are capable of being.*

—Johann Wolfgang von Goethe

Sometimes exceptional teachers, mentors, and coaches have a lasting beneficial effect on their students, trainees, or those they mentor. Those beneficiaries may, at some point, wish to acknowledge that support in writing. Likewise, exceptional performance on the part of certain students may warrant written praise or recommendation.

IMPORTANT: READ THIS BEFORE WRITING!

Although all the recipients described in this chapter will no doubt appreciate and even cherish these letters of appreciation, letter writers must be careful to observe the following legal precautions.

Some states or regions either have legislation or are considering adopting legislation that will severely penalize teachers who engage in *excess and inappropriate communication* with a student of any age within the public (and potentially private) school system. While this legislation has usually applied only to grades K–12, your state's legislation may be broader. *Before writing a letter of appreciation to a student or a teacher, conduct your due diligence on the matter and, if you deem it appropriate, consult an attorney.* Whether or not legislation exists in your state or region, teachers and students alike should use discretion. Even if the two of you are no longer in the same class, make sure the content and intent of your letter are fully consistent with an appropriate, educationally oriented teacher-student relationship.

If you take these and the other precautions mentioned in the rest of this chapter, your letter may make someone's day and even further the person's educational or career success.

TEACHERS

Do older or longtime teachers know their own worth? Do they realize the impact they've had on their students? Sometimes it takes years or decades for students to awaken to the many benefits they received from a particular teacher. Teachers give so much of themselves every day of their teaching career. You, in turn, can give something of yourself by sending your teacher a letter of appreciation.

Send your letter at the right time. If you're inspired by one of your current teachers, write your thoughts while he or she is fresh in your mind. Wait, however, to mail or present the letter until after the school year has ended and final grades have been turned in, so your letter won't be seen as an attempt to receive a better grade. Yes, this delay may present a challenge in reaching the teacher, but be imaginative in your quest: If the teacher is planning to teach a summer session after the spring term, you can still mail the letter to the teacher in care of the school. Otherwise, you can wait until the beginning of the next term when you know the teacher will have returned to school.

Track down your teacher's address. Email is the medium most students and much of the rest of the world are inclined to use because it's convenient. But consider how touched your teacher will be to know you took the trouble to write a thoughtful letter on nice stationery and mail it to his or her current address.

If the teacher is still teaching, the best plan is to mail it to the teacher in care of the school. If years have passed, call your school and ask at what school your teacher may now be reached so you can mail your letter directly. If you're writing to a college professor, go to RateMyProfessor.com, a nation-wide service, and type in the first and last name of the professor to find out where he or she is currently teaching. Then, look up the address of that college or university and send your letter there to the teacher's attention.

If your teacher is now retired, the school won't release the teacher's last known home address due to privacy concerns. Nevertheless, find out which school the teacher retired from and talk to office staff there about your challenge. Ask if they'd be willing to finish addressing a sealed, stamped envelope containing your letter if you mailed it to the school in a larger envelope along with a note repeating your request. Keep in mind they may be concerned if they can't first read and approve the content and thus may be unwilling to forward your letter. Even if you leave the envelope unsealed so they can read the content, you still have no assurance they will follow through. They may have a heavy workload or feel they shouldn't be held accountable because the teacher is no longer teaching. And even if the school *does* forward the letter, there's no way of knowing whether the teacher's last address in school files is still current and deliverable. All things considered, however, if this teacher had a significant influence on you, it's worth trying.

Of course, you can also search for the individual on the Internet and probably find the home address on your own. But, if possible, confirm that the address shown is current and complete (e.g., includes an apartment number, if required) before you mail the letter. Or ask one of your teacher's colleagues who may still keep in touch with him or her to see if there's a way to get your letter delivered. If the teacher's last name is uncommon, you could even employ an Internet search to help you locate relatives of the teacher who may be willing to help.

What to include in your letter. First, remind the teacher which of his or her classes you were in and when. If you're so inclined, you could even mention the names of some of your classmates at the time to provide context. Then, perhaps indicate which ones were your friends then and which ones you keep in touch with today.

Explain what inspired you to write:

♦ If you always looked forward to attending this class, describe why. What made it special?

♦ What positive qualities do you remember about this teacher? What, more than anything else, did you appreciate about him or her?

♦ What influence or lasting effect has his or her teaching style or content had on your life? Does it relate to your continuing education, your career, your marriage, your children, a special hobby, or your knack for fixing things around the house, in the garage, or in the car?

♦ Perhaps you remember this teacher for an entirely different reason—for catching you at bad behavior and handling it in a way that made you a better person today.

♦ Or maybe you became a teacher yourself because of this person's strong, positive example. If so, share that.

Near the end of your letter, repeat your appreciation for what the teacher did for you. Extend your best wishes, and optionally (if the person is not only local but retired), invite him or her to contact you to arrange a lunch out—your treat.

Somewhere in your letter (perhaps after your signature so it doesn't interrupt the flow of your letter), include your full name as the teacher would have known it then, full name today, current mailing address, email address, and phone number. This will make it easy for the teacher to contact you after receiving and reading your letter.

COACHES

When we think of coaches, we usually first think of sports coaches and trainers—coaches who help teams improve their performance at soccer, football, baseball, basketball, and so on. Included in this category are personal trainers who help individuals improve their sports skills or overall physical fitness.

But many other types of coaches exist as well:

- ◆ Life coaches help people achieve within both personal and professional spheres.
- ◆ Career coaches work with individuals to maximize their potential in their current or targeted career.
- ◆ Business coaches help people develop professionally and/or achieve success in their own company or business.
- ◆ Corporate coaches help align the values and professional goals of members of a corporation with the corporation's own vision, mission, and culture.
- ◆ Counselors within the fields of academia, social services, or psychology can also be considered coaches.

What do coaches all have in common? They facilitate positive change in the teams and individuals they coach. They do this by applying their experience and education in the best way they know how, to help others establish and achieve goals.

Did you ever have a special coach who made a big difference in your life, your team, your business, or your outlook? Do you have such a coach now? Your coach deserves to be appreciated. Write that letter now!

What to write to your coach. Begin by thanking your coach for the important role he or she has played in your life, and describe the positive and perhaps far-reaching results you have experienced due to his or her influence. Let some of these thoughts inspire you as you write:

> *Where would you have been today without your coach's positive influence?* What skills might you never have developed without his or her assistance? What classes or other educational opportunities might you never have availed yourself of, had it not been for him or her?

> *What roles have you played or positions have you held, thanks to your coach's influence?* In business, were you an owner, corporate vice president, facilitator, or public speaker? In the arts, were you a soloist, actor, musician, author, fine artist, or other artist? In sports and fitness, were you on a top team or did you occupy a key position or achieve a "personal best" in a particular area?

> *What special projects or achievements have the two of you accomplished together?*

> *How far reaching has your coach's influence been?* Are you now or do you plan to become a coach yourself? Are you already coaching others? How has your improved performance benefited your team,

company, or clients? In what other ways have you been able to share what you've learned?

End your letter with a sincere expression of your own gratitude, and add vicarious thanks from all the others upon whom your coach has also had a positive influence.

How and when to present your letter. The type of coach and the nature of your relationship will help determine *how* you'll want to present your letter. (Don't mail it, unless your relationship was long ago or it wouldn't be practical to visit personally.) As to *when*, the following times are propitious:

- Sports—the end of the season
- Personal fitness training—upon achieving a personal fitness milestone
- Business—at the end of a great fiscal year
- Career coaching—after achieving a coveted position

If you're an athlete writing to a non-school-related coach, pick any time or circumstance you deem appropriate for your personal presentation. However, if you're a student athlete writing to your coach, wait to mail or present the letter until after the school year has ended and final grades or other assessments have been turned in. That way, your letter won't be misconstrued as seeking favored treatment. This delay may present a challenge in reaching the coach, but be imaginative. If the coach plans to teach a summer session after the spring term, you can still mail the letter to the coach in care of the school after spring term. Otherwise, you could wait until the beginning of the next term, when you know the coach will have returned to school.

MENTORS

Mentors are a bit different from coaches because they haven't received money for their valuable services. It may be that you asked for a mentor relationship, or perhaps your mentor made the offer. Or the two of you may have fallen into the mentoring relationship over time and never even used the word *mentor*. Regardless, your mentor has served as your guide to encourage you, expand your horizons, and keep nudging you (and sometimes pushing you hard) out of your comfort zone and into opportunities in which you could more fully realize your potential. The mentoring may relate to work, volunteerism, or another professional arena.

The purpose of your letter is to acknowledge your mentor for the important role he or she has played in your life and describe the far-reaching, positive consequences that have resulted from the relationship. Your letter will serve to validate your mentor's efforts and make him or her more aware of having achieved part of his or her life's purpose.

Let your writing be inspired by these thoughts:

> *Where would you be today without your mentor's positive influence?* What types of activities might you never have tried or become involved in? What skills might you never have explored or developed? What classes or other educational opportunities might you never have availed yourself of?

> *What roles have you played or positions have you held, thanks to your mentor's influence:* Public speaker? Business owner? Corporate vice president? PTA president? Event coordinator? Facilitator? Soloist? Actor? Musician? Author?

> *What special projects have the two of you accomplished together?*

How far reaching is your mentor's influence? Are you now or do you plan to become a teacher? Are you mentoring others? How have your efforts as a now-experienced volunteer benefited others? In what other ways have you been able to "pay it forward"?

End your letter with a sincere expression of gratitude, and add vicarious thanks from all the others your mentor has influenced in a positive way.

How to present your letter. Present your letter during a special appreciation meal out—just the two of you (your treat).

STUDENTS

Many students work hard at their education and therefore are high achievers. Sometimes they receive a scholarship or other special honor or award that inspires others to offer greater congratulations or appreciation than a greeting card alone can convey. Time to write a heartfelt letter!

If you're the student's parent(s), peer, or friend, begin by congratulating the student for earning the honor or award, or by declaring your admiration. Then write one or more paragraphs about the positive academic traits you have observed over time and include a couple of examples. In another paragraph, express your high expectations for the student's ongoing achievement based on past performance and what you know about his or her persevering qualities. Then, in a final paragraph, express your support as the student continues his or her education.

If you're the student's current or former teacher, *first read the important cautions on the first page of this chapter* to help you decide *whether* to write such a letter. Then, if you choose to proceed, regardless of your letter's purpose, never write anything that could be misconstrued by anyone as indicating or inviting an inappropriate teacher/student relationship.

In your first paragraph, explain briefly what inspired you to write, whether it's congratulations for an award or other honor, a recommendation, or just sincere admiration. In the next paragraph, describe a few of the student's academic qualities and positive character traits you most admire, and perhaps cite a couple of circumstances you can recall in which these qualities or traits were demonstrated.

In the final paragraph, express confidence that these traits will continue to serve the student well in the academic arena, as well as in life. If this is a congratulatory letter for an award or honor, restate those congratulations here in different words and say you're honored to be associated academically with the student.

When and how to present your letter. If you're the student's current teacher, the timing of your letter depends on its purpose. If the intention of your letter is to express congratulations on a special award or scholarship, don't delay. Present your letter personally or mail it to the student's home. If it's a letter of reference, respond quickly but thoughtfully, with guidance found under Letter of Reference (Recommendation Letter) in the Career chapter within Part 2. But if you plan to write a general letter based on genuine admiration for a prized student's academic ethic, wait to mail it until after the current school term has ended and grades have already been submitted. Similarly, if you're a school coach writing to your student athlete, wait until after the season or school term has ended to mail your letter.

Look up the student's current mailing address and mail the letter at the appropriate time, using the *school's* address in the return address block of both the letter and the envelope. Don't divulge your own address.

HONORING A SPECIAL FRIENDSHIP

Make new friends, but keep the old.
One is silver and the other gold.

—Unknown

Whatever would we do without good friends? If you'd like to celebrate your friendship with a special friend, a letter of appreciation is the perfect way to do it, and you'll have plenty to write about.

What to write in your letter. How did your friendship develop? What first made you want to be his or her friend? What has typified your friendship so far? What benefits do or will these qualities bring to your life?

You can mention specific treasured memories if space permits. These questions may spark memories for you:

- ♦ What especially fun times have you enjoyed together?
- ♦ What was your most embarrassing moment together?
- ♦ Did the two of you ever build or cook something together? How did that go?
- ♦ Did you sing songs or play instruments together? Does a particular song evoke a funny, joyful, or poignant situation for the two of you?

- ◆ What leisure activities—picnics, camping, boating, reading, golfing, bike riding, plays/musicals, games or gaming, sports, amusement parks— have brought you closer as friends? What made these experiences special to you?

- ◆ Have you taken any day trips or extended road trips together? What were those like? What positive or humorous memories do you have from them?

- ◆ Do you want to allude to any inside secrets or inside jokes you share?

Describe how the relationship with your friend has affected your life. For example:

How are the two of you most alike? How are you most different? What qualities do you most admire about your friend? What do your family and other friends especially like about him or her? What is he or she best known for among your friends? Did you experience a hardship that your friend helped you overcome? How does your friend respond in a crisis? Is it with efficiency, selflessness, fast or considered action, or some other beneficial quality?

How have you become a better person because of your friendship? Has your friend "opened doors" for you, thus enhancing your life? What positive effect has your friend had on your life? What positive effect have you had on your friend's life?

Share how you see your friendship continuing to blossom and perhaps how you can achieve dreams together. What is it about the two of you that best indicates your future happiness and success together as friends? In what way will you or do you especially appreciate being with him or her? *Make this the strongest part of your letter.*

Ideas on presenting your letter. Present your letter on your friend's birthday or during a special appreciation luncheon at a fine restaurant—or at your place, and serve a wonderful homemade meal for just the two of you.

Write your heartfelt letter of appreciation but consider this suggestion as an additional way to celebrate your friendship: If your friend gave you a gift long ago that you've continued to enjoy, send a thank you note every few years saying how much that gift still means to you. Say that you think of him or her fondly every time you use, read, or enjoy the gift.

Thanking a Product Creator or Stellar Service Provider

Quality begins on the inside...
and then works its way out.

—Bob Moawad

Have you ever been extremely impressed with a new product you purchased? Have you ever had a personal service performed for you in an exceptional way—from house-cleaning to gardening to a great massage? Has your own company or your employer ever received a superior level of service by an outside contractor? Have you ever had a problem with a purchase transaction, product, or service that was resolved by the company, manufacturer, or service provider in a highly effective "going the extra mile" way? Has an individual, colleague, or business associate brought your business several new clients or customers over a period of months or years?

Sometimes product, service, problem solving, and business-referral experiences are so outstanding that we want to not only tell our friends or business associates but also thank the source. And a heartfelt letter does just that.

Simple Business-Letter Structure

If you're a consumer rather than a business owner or employee, you may be unfamiliar with the traditional format for a typed business letter. This simple, top-to-bottom, line-by-line guide should help. Start everything from the left-hand margin to keep it simple:

> Your street address or post office box (if not using company stationery)
> Your city, state/province/territory, and zip/postal code (if not using company stationery)
> Today's date
> *[At least 2 blank lines]*
> Recipient's name (No need to precede with Mr. or Ms. here, but MD, PhD, DDS, etc. may be appropriate after the name, if it's relevant to the reason you're writing)
> Title (if any)
> Department (if any)
> Company or practice name (if any)
> Street address or post office box
> City, state/province/territory, and zip/postal code
> *[1 blank line]*
> Optional subject line; for example:
> > Subject: A Glowing Report on XYZ Product
> *[1 blank line, only if including a subject line]*
> Salutation, using a colon instead of a comma after the name; for example:
> > Dear Ms. Logathetti:
> *[1 blank line]*
> First paragraph
> *[1 blank line]*
> Second and each additional intervening paragraph
> *[1 blank line after each paragraph]*
> Last paragraph
> *[1 blank line]*

Complimentary close, with only the first word
   capitalized, ending in a comma (for example:
   Sincerely, In gratitude, Always,)

[3 blank lines, where you'll later sign in ink]

Your full typewritten name
Optional department name (if writing as a business)
Optional telephone number (if you choose to
   divulge it)

[1 blank line]

List of others to whom you're sending copies;
   for example:

    cc: John Jones, Supervisor, Customer Service
          Mary Smith, Manager, Human Resources

SUPERIOR PRODUCTS

Every now and then, a product comes along whose features, benefits, or overall quality are so remarkable that you're moved to send more than a brief thank-you note to the individual or company responsible. When companies receive letters that compliment them or their products, those letters are treasured. The companies often display them or quote from them in communications with employees and other customers. If you write one, make it your very best effort.

Who should receive your letter? Track down the person most appropriate to write to. It will probably be the president or CEO of the company. Then, depending on what you like about the product, you may decide to send a duplicate copy to the head of another department, such as sales, marketing, research and development, or quality assurance.

What to write in your letter. Start your letter by explaining you're a purchaser of ABC product. If it's a product you buy often, such as food, bath soap, vitamins, three-ring binders, or pens, say how long you've been using it. If you recently started using the product and were immediately impressed, write that instead, perhaps mentioning how you first learned about it.

Then explain the product's single most important feature that impressed you. Depending on the product, it might be ease of use, appealing taste, pleasant scent, deep-cleaning capability, beautiful color, durability, nice fit—you get the idea. In what way has that feature had a positive effect on your personal or business life—that is, how has it benefited you? Do you feel happier, more energized, less fatigued? Are your meals tastier or more satisfying? Do you look nicer? Does your house or your office look better or operate more efficiently? Again, your answer here depends on the product and how you use it in your personal or business environment.

Next, describe what else you like about the product—in each case, name the feature and then tell how it has benefited you or your business.

If possible, say how you've told others about the product. Perhaps you've recommended it to friends or associates personally, posted a product review on the manufacturer's website or a consumer evaluation website, or made complimentary remarks about the product and/or company to your social media contacts.

Conclude your letter by pledging your loyalty to the product and/or the company.

Ideas on presenting your letter. Mail the original letter and any duplicate copies in separate, individually addressed envelopes; don't bunch them all into the same envelope.

STELLAR SERVICE

Sometimes a personal or business service provider so far exceeds expectations that you want to do something special in return. So send a letter expressing your appreciation!

Who should receive your letter? In every instance, write to the service provider. *If that provider is a freelancer* (not a subcontractor or employee of another company) who provides either a personal service such as massage, landscaping, or housecleaning or a business service such as copywriting, virtual assistance, or consulting, you need send only the original letter.

But if the provider is a subcontractor, performing the service on behalf of another company that considers you its own client, be sure to send a copy of your letter to the company representative the provider reports to. That way, he or she is alerted to the subcontractor's value.

Or, if the provider is the employee of a company, send a copy of your letter to the immediate supervisor to make him or her more aware of the employee's value. And send another copy to the company's Human Resources department, where it can be placed in the employee's official personnel file.

What to write in your letter. Start by explaining how long or for what project you've been working with the provider, explaining the nature of the service that you've received. (While the service provider already knows this, put it in writing anyway for the sake of completeness and to clarify the service relationship for all those who receive copies of the letter.) If you recently started using the service and were immediately impressed, mention that, too. It would also be appropriate to say how you learned of the service or service provider.

Next, explain who (the service provider) or what (for example, the company's policies, customer service, etc.) has impressed you, starting with the most important aspect. Go into detail, and give examples. Discuss how you've benefited from the service provided, being as specific as you can.

To get that detail, ask yourself these types of questions, as applicable:

- ♦ How much better do you feel after working with this product or service?
- ♦ How are you able to perform your job more efficiently because of it?
- ♦ By what percent have sales increased (or are sales likely to increase)?
- ♦ How much more competitive is your business than it was?
- ♦ How has your professional image improved?
- ♦ How much better does your (house, yard, etc.) look?
- ♦ How does that make you feel?

If others at the service provider's company have also treated you well, mention their names. Remember to send copies of your letter to them also.

In the next paragraph, if applicable, state your feeling that this service provider or service company enjoys a competitive advantage, due largely to the efforts of the individual(s) you've just described.

To help demonstrate the far-reaching rewards to a service provider for a job well done, explain the ways in which you've recommended the service to others. Perhaps you've spoken highly of the service to friends or associates personally; you've posted a testimonial of the service on the website of the freelance service provider, primary contracting company, or employer; or you've made complimentary remarks about the product and/or company to your social media contacts.

Conclude your letter by pledging your loyalty to the service provider and (if applicable) to the primary contracting company or employer.

Ideas on presenting your letter. You will probably mail your letter; if so, mail the original letter and any duplicate copies in separate, individually addressed envelopes; don't put them all into the same envelope. Or you could instead present it flat or folded in an envelope during a thank-you lunch; but still mail any copies you are distributing to others.

EFFECTIVE PROBLEM RESOLUTION

It seems everyone has experienced a significant problem with a product or service. Sometimes when these problems are handled poorly by the company or service provider, consumers remain unhappy and tell others about their unpleasant experience. Other times, problems are resolved satisfactorily. And still other times, the problem resolutions are handled so well, they exceed the consumers' hopes and expectations. That inspires the consumers to tell others how well they were treated.

If that last situation has happened to you, then besides talking with your friends and posting your positive experience on a consumer-advocate or social-media site, you might feel moved to write a letter of thanks to the company, manufacturer, or service provider.

Who should receive your letter? Your letter should be addressed to the individual who resolved your problem. If your problem and resolution related to a freelance service provider or one-person business, then clearly this will be the only individual to receive that letter. Otherwise, when deciding who else should receive a copy of that letter, apply the Golden Rule by imagining what the person who resolved your problem would prefer.

♦ *If the nature of the problem and its resolution
  are something your contact would prefer to keep
  confidential* between the two of you, write only
  to that person.

♦ *If your contact was a subcontractor* to another firm
  that functioned as the primary contracting
  company, send a copy to the contracting
  company's representative to whom your
  contact reported.

♦ *If your contact was the employee originally responsible
  for selling you the product or service,* send a copy
  to his or her supervisor and another copy to the
  Human Resources department for placement
  in the employee's personnel file.

♦ *If your problem-resolution contact was a customer
  service representative,* send a copy to his or her
  supervisor and, if applicable, another to the person
  who sold you the product or service. Again, you
  could send a copy to the Human Resources
  department for inclusion in the employee's
  personnel file.

What to write in your letter. Start your letter by thanking
your contact for selling you ABC product or providing
XYZ service, mentioning the approximate date the transaction took place. Then describe briefly the type of problem
you encountered.

Next—and this is the most important part of your letter—
describe how, specifically, your contact resolved the problem
and met or exceeded your expectations. Was efficiency,
selflessness, speed, considered action, or something else
involved in the resolution? Say so with specifics. And if others
at the company besides the service provider also treated you
well in the process, mention their names and remember to
send copies of your letter to them as well.

State how pleased you were with the resolution. Then you can conclude your letter by telling your contact that, as a result of his or her efforts, instead of being unhappy and telling others about what might otherwise have been a bad experience, you are now a loyal fan who is enthusiastically telling others what a great company (or service provider) you've had the pleasure to deal with.

Ideas on presenting your letter. Mail the original letter and any duplicate copies in separate, individually addressed envelopes; don't bunch them all into the same envelope.

STAR REFERRAL SOURCES

Do you know someone who regularly recommends your professional services or products or who has been the referral source for one of your biggest clients or customers? Instead of the usual thank-you *note* of the type you surely send to colleagues, business associates, clients, or customers for each new client or customer, you may want to do something extra special to acknowledge your wonderful referral source, and a business thank-you *letter* could be just the thing.

Who should receive your letter? Write your letter to the individual, such as a customer, client, or colleague, who regularly makes these referrals. But if this is a business relationship in which most or all employees within a certain company's department regularly refer business to you, send your letter to the department supervisor with a request to share its contents with all the department's employees.

What to write in your letter. If you're writing to your client or customer, start your letter by thanking the person for past business or patronage. Then especially thank him or her for regularly recommending you to others. If you can, name some of the people who have become your customers or clients as a result of those referrals, and tell how much you enjoy assisting them with their needs. Explain that word of mouth is the most important and meaningful way to grow a business or clientele; these new individuals are inclined to be more loyal and committed due to the referring party's expression of confidence in you. Conclude your letter by repeating your thanks for the business and for his or her kindness in making referrals. Let the person know you're ready to be of service in return.

If you're writing to a colleague in the same business category as you, start your letter by thanking the colleague for regularly recommending you to others. If you can, name people who have become your customers or clients as a result of those referrals, saying how much you enjoy assisting them with their needs. Note that word of mouth helps grow a business or clientele, and that referred people are inclined to be more loyal. Thank the referring party for putting his or her reputation on the line by expressing confidence in you. Repeat your thanks for ongoing referrals and say you'll be happy to reciprocate when possible.

If you're writing to a business associate in a synergistic business (for example, writing to a real estate agent who refers new home buyers to your landscape-maintenance service), start by thanking the associate for recommending you to others. If you can, name those who have become your customers or clients as a result of those referrals. Express how much you enjoy assisting them with their needs. Mention that word of mouth is the most important way to grow a client base. Conclude by repeating your thanks for the continuing referrals, letting your associate know you'll be happy to reciprocate when appropriate.

Ideas on presenting your letter. You will probably mail your letter, but you could instead present it flat or in an envelope during a thank-you lunch.

BRINGING MEANING TO
A LIFE WELL LIVED

We will be known forever by the tracks we leave.

—Dakota proverb

Most people, especially as they grow older, want to believe they have made a positive difference in their world. Maybe they've been a loving spouse or parent, grown good crops, been kind to animals, volunteered in worthwhile causes, taught or mentored others, represented a strong example to friends and co-workers, given wise counsel, helped patients with their medical needs or clients with their goals, conducted important research, invented a useful product—the possibilities are nearly infinite.

Much of this chapter focuses on helping others realize, through a letter of appreciation, that indeed they have made a positive difference. That realization helps give their life meaning. Do write and deliver that letter soon, because life can be fleeting.

But even if people have died, it's still important to honor them and their legacy. You can do this by writing and delivering a eulogy or brief public tribute. Alternatively, you can write a more personal letter and deliver it as part of a more private or personal observance. This chapter offers several ways you can do that.

AGING RELATIVES AND FRIENDS

As we see our friends and loved ones age, we become aware that their time with us may be more limited than we'd like. We may start having regrets, such as "Why didn't we ever get around to...?" or "Why didn't I ever say...?" Or musings, such as "I hope he knows how much he means to me" or "I really should tell her more often that I love her." We can't change the past, but we can certainly do something about the present, not only by modifying our behavior for the better but by giving those dear to us the gift of a letter of appreciation.

What to write in your letter. Regardless of your relationship, say you're thinking of the person and love and/or appreciate him or her. Describe happy memories you recall. Mention positive qualities and perhaps give examples of when the person expressed these qualities. We all want to feel we've had a positive impact on others, so describe the impact he or she has had on your life and on the lives of others as you've observed firsthand or been told by others.

And then:

♦ *If you're the spouse or significant other,* also mention challenges you've weathered together and how you both learned or came out stronger for the experience. Write about the legacy he or she has left through your children (if you have any), briefly mentioning the positive qualities and other things that make you proud of each of them. Remind your partner that you have been and always will be devoted to him or her. And end your letter with an expression of love.

♦ *If you're a brother or sister,* also recall childhood games you played together or sports, hobbies, or other activities you both enjoyed. Relate a funny incident, if you want. Write about challenging times growing up together and how you both learned or came out stronger for the experience. Describe what you've always admired about your sibling, and explain what you like about your relationship today. End your letter by expressing your love in whatever way comes most naturally to you.

♦ *If you're a son or daughter,* also tell about his or her positive parenting style you experienced as a child and how that helped you become who you are today. Along those lines, describe any disciplinary actions you recall that may have helped you grow from the experience. Tell about sports, hobbies, or other activities you shared. If your parent was an active volunteer in team sports or any school or community activities in which you were involved, say how proud you were of his or her efforts. Describe how your parent-child relationship has matured over the years and what it's like today. For example, are you good friends today, or do you still seek advice from time to time? End your letter by expressing your love.

♦ *If you're a niece, nephew, or grandchild,* also tell what you enjoyed about his or her company in your childhood. Describe how your relationship has evolved over the years into what it is today. For example, are you good friends today, or do you still ask his or her advice from time to time? Write about sports (even spectator sports), hobbies, or other activities or interests you have shared or have in common. End your letter by expressing your affection and love.

♦ *If you're a friend,* and you've known each other most of your lives, also recall games you played together when you were younger or sports (even spectator sports), hobbies, or other activities (even shopping or having a pleasurable lunch out) you have enjoyed together over the years. Relate a funny incident, if you want. Tell about any challenging times you may have helped each other through. Describe what you've always admired about your friend, and say what you like about your relationship today. End your letter by expressing your genuine affection.

How to present your letter. If he or she is bedridden, present your letter personally and privately during a visit—perhaps bringing cookies or another treat as well. If your letter is for the guest of honor at a party or banquet and it could be read aloud at the event without embarrassing the recipient, then read it aloud there. Otherwise, present your letter gift wrapped or in a large, attractive envelope for the person to read privately at the event or afterwards. If no special event is slated, arrange one for just the two of you in an environment in which you're both comfortable—on a front porch, in a sunroom, in a garden or park, or at a favorite restaurant.

PATIENTS IN HOSPICE CARE

When you learn that someone dear is dying, it's natural to feel sad for the person and sad for your own anticipated loss. At a time like this, people react differently. Some avoid the dying person because they don't know what to say or how to act, whereas others hurry to the bedside to show their love and support. Above all, remember that the hospice care period is a wonderful opportunity to enrich relationships while you still can.

If hospice patients are mentally aware, they certainly know they're dying. Patients sometimes find this to be a time of quiet contemplation of pleasant memories, rewarding relationships, and their legacy soon to be left behind. This legacy may be in the form of children, grandchildren, past students, a wonderful marriage partnership, or the like. Other times, hospice patients find themselves laughing and joking with family and friends and others who come to visit. Either way, they're making this stage of life as meaningful and filled with quality experiences as possible. In most cases, that means treasuring their time with loved ones and reminiscing about the good times they've had.

In *Love & Death: My Journey Through the Valley of the Shadow* (Beacon Press, 2008), Forrest Church, himself terminally ill at the time, wrote, "... The purpose of life is to live in such a way that our lives will prove worth dying for." So in these final days, weeks, or months, the focus tends to be on love and legacy.

One of the best ways to give of yourself to your dying loved one or friend when it really counts is to visit in person. Holding a hand, giving a smile, sharing a joke or a memory all mean so much. Whether or not you visit personally, another powerful way to help the dying person know that he or she has made a positive difference in the world is to write a letter of reminiscence and appreciation. A letter of any length can elicit a peaceful smile every time it's read.

What to write in your letter. The most important things to express are that the person is in your thoughts and you love him or her. People also want to know they've made a positive difference in their lifetimes—that they've left a legacy. So describe the important role this person has played in your own life. What have you learned personally from this person, whether it was from his or her outright teaching or example? How has he or she made you a better person? Describe any other important life lessons you may have learned from this individual and how following those lessons made your life better or easier, or improved your relationships with others.

Even the little things count. Did this person teach you to appreciate a free afternoon or a sunset? Do you remember tasting his or her homemade chocolate-chip cookies warm from the oven, or smelling that wonderful vegetable soup simmering on the stove? If it's your parent who is dying, do you have fond memories of feeling safe and loved by him or her when you were tucked into bed with a bedtime story and a kiss?

Also help the individual become aware of the positive impact he or she has had on others besides you. What did the person teach others, or what did others learn by the person's example? Describe how the individual's legacy will live on in the hearts, minds, or lives of others who knew him or her.

Some people find it difficult to summarize the enormity of a person's life, so they don't write or visit at all. Don't let this be you, because it will deprive both you and your loved one of an enriching and possibly even uplifting experience. At the very least, let the person know he or she is in your thoughts.

What to avoid writing or saying. Don't say things are going to get better, and avoid expressions such as "God has a plan," "You'll soon be at rest," "Soon you'll be with the angels," and so on. Instead, speak or write in terms of the past as well as the here and now; focus on what he or she contributed rather than the future. Don't try to explain why someone is going through this pain or process of dying or say "There's a reason for this." Rather than address the unknown or try to soothe the person with platitudes, bring up something pleasant in the person's past or present experience that will warm his or her heart.

How to present your letter. Your presentation will vary depending on circumstances. Can you be there personally? Is he or she able to hear or read what you've written? Would he or she like you to read the letter aloud or leave it so someone else can read it aloud later? Use your instincts and good judgment in this regard.

THOSE DEAR TO HOSPICE PATIENTS

We enter the sacred realm of the heart, where the one thing that can never be taken from us, even by death, is the love we give away before we go.

—Forrest Church, *Love and Death: My Journey through the Valley of the Shadow* (Beacon Press, 2008)

Hospice gives patients the opportunity to finish the business of living. *If you're a hospice patient*, it's a good time to share what you've learned on life's journey:

♦ Tell or retell memories and stories from earlier in life that will be passed along to future generations;

♦ Reflect on and express gratitude for valued and loving relationships or assistance given through life;

♦ Make an effort to rebuild damaged relationships through asking for and expressing forgiveness.

If you're physically and mentally able, all these things can be spoken during informal visits, conveyed through audio recordings, or written down as heartfelt letters. Indeed, you may be enthusiastic about leaving these messages. You may direct them to your spouse, children, and unborn children if you're younger, or to your spouse, adult children, grandchildren, and great-grandchildren if you're older.

What to share in person, write in your letter, or say in your recording. You can offer thoughts about what's been important to you and other life lessons: "If I only knew then what I know now...." You can talk about shared memories. Even a small, heartfelt memory or a short reflection can mean so much when shared. You can let someone else know why he or she has been appreciated in your life. To validate the role the other person has played is a powerful thing to do. All these activities add to your legacy and will be appreciated by those you leave behind.

This is not the time to try to "settle a score," but it *is* the perfect time to be forgiving and to ask forgiveness, as this can bring great emotional healing and peace.

> *A few words of advice for the loved ones nearest the hospice patient:* Hospice caregivers suggest that if a torn relationship exists within the family, such as a son and father who haven't spoken in years, and one of them is dying, you may *gently encourage* the dying person to forgive or ask forgiveness. Or you may suggest some other positive, simple gesture to help heal the relationship, such as writing a simple note or making a phone call. But *don't try to force a dying person to do something he or she is not ready to do.*

How to present your letter or recording. Your circumstances, as well as your recipient's ability to visit you, will help determine whether to save your letter for the next visit or go ahead and mail it. If your recipient is coming for a visit, you may present your letter in a sealed or unsealed envelope and state your preference as to whether you'd like him or her to read it during the visit or at a later time. If it's an audio recording, the option to listen at the time or later on is also a preference you can state. If your recipient is unable to come for a visit, you can mail your letter or audio recording. If the audio recording is digital, it can be transmitted as an email attachment or by FTP (file transfer protocol) service, or copied to a flash drive and mailed.

Whenever you're transmitting important letters or other communications, use a reliable mailing method. Also take the precaution to photocopy or otherwise duplicate these items before mailing or emailing in case something is lost while in transit.

EULOGIES AND PUBLIC TRIBUTES

When a person dies, a memorial service or funeral service usually takes place. During that service, often someone delivers a 10- to 20-minute eulogy, or talk. Alternatively, a 5- to 10-minute official eulogy is given followed by a "time of remembrance," during which several others present offer preplanned or spontaneous 2- to 3-minute public tributes.

How to write and deliver a eulogy. The eulogy can be delivered by a member of the clergy or a close friend or relative, either referring to notes or reading word for word. Its purpose is to provide a kind and respectful message of love for the deceased and to tell stories or give examples explaining why those present share that love.

Quality, not quantity. If you're delivering the eulogy, its quality is more important than its length; still, you may want to ask the family how long they'd like the eulogy to be; then do your best to comply.

Try to establish a theme. It can be:

♦ A question ("What was George Miller really like?");

♦ A quotation that inspires a theme ("Always do right; this will gratify some people and astonish the rest." —Mark Twain);

♦ A metaphor ("Priscilla's life was like a sweet dream, filled with a zest for life"); or

♦ Alliteration ("Eugene was cantankerous, caring, and courageous").

The theme helps tie together the disparate parts of the deceased individual's life, which you'll be describing.

If you're unable to establish a theme initially, you may find a theme emerging on its own as you decide what to say and what stories to tell. If you never do come up with a theme, people won't mind, as long as you deliver the information sincerely and cohesively.

Gather stories and memories. Talk with friends, relatives, and co-workers, and also recall your own firsthand accounts to gather stories that support your theme or best illustrate the life of the deceased. Include humor if it's part of a story, but keep it in good taste; don't include anything else that is in poor taste or would have embarrassed the person being honored. If the family of the deceased isn't too large, find a way to mention every family member so they'll all feel appreciated.

Sometimes it can be challenging to find good things to say about the deceased, no matter how many people you talk to who knew him or her. So rather than speak untruths, a refreshingly honest approach to consider is to preface some of your remarks with "Let's face it..." or "Let's be honest...," as long as these remarks are made with kindness and respect.

As you write the eulogy, use your normal vocabulary and tone. That way, the delivery will seem more natural, as if you're speaking informally. Yet it's important to stay on topic and avoid rambling, too. If that means referring to detailed notes or reading the eulogy word for word, so be it.

Organize the eulogy in a logical sequence. Begin with an introduction in which you first thank people for coming to honor (or celebrate) the life of the deceased. Acknowledge that each person present knew the deceased from a unique perspective, be it as family member, relative, friend, fellow student, or co-worker. State that even though participants may not know one another, they're united today because they all cared about him or her. Then establish your theme and explain how you knew the deceased (unless you are someone who gathered information and didn't know the deceased personally). If you did know the deceased, perhaps begin with an opening firsthand story to demonstrate what made the deceased or your relationship with him or her special to you. If relevant, you could describe how the individual had a profound impact on your own life or on the lives of others.

Follow this with the body of the talk, telling stories and describing memories. You may decide to include one or two favorite quotations of the deceased and talk about why they were meaningful to him or her. Somewhere in this process, interject a bit of humor, whether it's an inside joke or a behavioral characteristic that most of the attendees will recall with affection.

Then give a conclusion, in which you summarize what was special about the deceased and how he or she touched the lives of others. Finally, thank the audience for attending and remind them they're here for each other. Say that after the service, if they want to talk and feel comforted, they need only look around the room for others who are available to them and will also appreciate being comforted.

Be critical of the content as you rehearse. Does everything make sense? Have you included enough detail, but not too much? Have you avoided profanity or slander? Did you take care not to discuss your personal pain at the loss? (The eulogy is your gift to the audience; it's already understood that you, too, are grieving if you knew the deceased.) Do you mention yourself too much? Have you taken care not to imply that grieving will end soon or on any particular timetable? (Grieving is, after all, a highly personal journey.) Were you careful to avoid such expressions as "He's in a better place now" or "She's better off now"? (These types of statements unfairly diminish the finality, seriousness, and pain of the loss.)

Strive to shed all your tears before or during rehearsals so you can successfully complete your delivery at the service. But do designate an alternate who can deliver or continue the eulogy in the event you cannot.

Before the service begins, arrange to have a glass of water accessible where you'll be speaking. No one will mind if you need to take an occasional sip.

Just before you deliver your eulogy, take a few slow, deep breaths to relax your mind and remove tension.

As you deliver your eulogy, speak slowly and clearly. If you have no microphone, project your voice so you can be heard in the back of the room. If you start to lose your composure, pause briefly and take a sip of water before continuing. (If you're unable to continue, signal to your alternate to take your place and read the remainder of the eulogy.) When you're finished speaking, thank the audience, and then sit down.

Although presenting a slide show may be a bit over the top, one or two small visual aids can add something positive to help make your point. For example, you might hold up a baseball when talking about Jerry's coaching Little League, or hold up the Rubik's Cube that Melanie always kept on her desk and fiddled with while talking on the phone.

At some point after the service, make the rare but appreciated gesture of giving a copy of the eulogy to the family as a memento or remembrance. And mark your calendar for the one-year anniversary of the individual's date of death. Just before that anniversary, send a note to family and friends who were closest to the deceased, saying you're thinking of them at this time and you still remember the deceased with fondness. It will mean a great deal to them. You could even call to suggest getting together to toast his or her memory.

How to write and deliver a brief oral tribute. Read the preceding section on eulogies, as most of that advice applies to a brief oral tribute, but on a smaller scale. It's better to read your tribute word for word or refer to your notes, but if you decide to speak impromptu, take care not to ramble or speak longer than intended.

> You'll feel better if you get up and say something than if you just sit there and don't, but want to. Don't feel intimidated or let a fear of public speaking control you. Nobody will judge your public speaking skills in this situation if you're speaking from the heart.

Tell a story; make a point about the deceased that will help others appreciate him or her; but don't use this forum just to say, "I'll miss her, too." Don't take this opportunity to "settle a score" with the deceased either, as no one will appreciate it, and you will lose respect. Avoid profanity or slander. While it's all right to tell a funny story, don't say anything that would have embarrassed the deceased.

Keep your tribute brief to give others a forum, too; then sit down when you're finished speaking.

Consider writing a eulogy for yourself. More people are starting to write their own eulogies while they're still in good health as an opportunity to leave a legacy for others. What better forum for sharing your values and thoughts the way you'd like them delivered?

If you decide to write your own eulogy, make sure multiple family members know where you're keeping it so they can find it readily when you die. You might want to keep a legacy binder. In this binder, you can store your eulogy and preferences as to music, favorite charity, and type and tenor of funeral or memorial service. You can include written or recorded accounts of memories you treasure so others will know more about you and what you found valuable in life.

PERSONAL LETTERS TO DECEASED FRIENDS AND LOVED ONES

Note: Some activities and suggestions within this section may tie in with observances for two special occasions covered in Part 2: Memorial Day, in the Military chapter; and Día de los Muertos (also known as Day of the Dead), discussed under Ancestral Rites in the chapter Cultural and Religious Rites of Passage. So as you envision what you want to write in your letter and how you want to present it, refer to those sections, too.

Friends and loved ones may have died, but they still exist in your heart. How do you feel about them today? If need be, it's never too late to promote healing between you and the one who has died. You may want to write out and read aloud any feelings of grief, resentment, or regret you wish to release. This ceremony can help you remember the person more fondly, progress through your grieving, heal any resentment, and lay to rest any lingering regrets.

What to write in your letter. As you contemplate what to include in your letter, consider whether you plan to share the contents of your letter with one or more other friends or relatives who were dear to the deceased. Sharing is appropriate only if your letter focuses on love and appreciation exclusively, it isn't highly intimate, and you believe others would treasure the letter. Alternatively, give yourself permission to write whatever you're feeling, knowing that your letter will be seen and read only by you. After you've written and read it, you can ceremoniously release it, then destroy it or store it where it will never be discovered by others.

In a letter of appreciation, write how much you miss him or her. Reminisce about good times you shared and challenges you overcame together. Even the little things count: Remember how Julia taught you how to meditate while commuting on the subway? Remember tasting Aunt Ruby's wonderful home-made chocolate pies? Remember the aroma of Uncle Tony's fresh, handmade tortillas cooking on the griddle? How about fishing with Granddad during spring weekends when he'd always get all the bites except the ones from mosquitoes? Remember the rainy days when you and your sister Linda built indoor caves using furniture, tray tables, and blankets, and then crawled inside and ate soda crackers with butter?

Describe the traits you always admired or loved about the person you miss. What role did your friend Gillian play in your own life? What did you learn personally from Uncle John, whether from outright teaching or from observing the example he set? How did Cousin Francine make you a better person?

Describe any other important life lessons you may have learned from the person you miss. How did following those lessons make your life better or easier, or improve your relationships with others? What did the person teach others, or what did others learn through his or her example? Describe how this person's legacy will live on in the hearts, minds, or lives of other people.

End your letter with an expression of gratitude and affection or love.

In a highly personal, perhaps even therapeutic letter, you may want to write about whatever is troubling you relating to the deceased:

> Are you still grieving at some level? Are you hurting over the loss? Do you miss him or her? When do you feel most lonely or empty? Do you feel relieved that the person's suffering has ended? Do you find peace in the belief that this person is now in a better place?

On the other hand, are you angry because you feel you've been abandoned? Are you feeling wounded or resentful regarding something that happened or didn't happen in the past between you and the person who died? Do you regret something that was or wasn't said or done between you? In other words, do you and the deceased have unfinished business?

Even as an adult, for example, you may still feel wounded by an incident or circumstance when you were growing up, relating to something your parents said or did, or something you feel they shouldn't have said or done. Or if your parents were divorced and at least one of them is now deceased, during the divorce you may have felt hurt, abandoned, ignored, unloved, or unsupported because, at the time, your parents were unhappy and involved in their own problems.

What if you're the parent of a child who has died? The hurt of outliving your child can be almost unimaginable. Here, you'd probably write a love letter to your child, describing all the ways he or she was treasured and considered a blessing in your life. However, if on some level you also feel abandoned because your child died, it's okay to express that, too.

Once you've written to the deceased individual explaining how you feel, write a second letter—this time from the point of view of the person who has died, as if he or she were writing to you. This can represent the letter you wish the person would have written to you when you were a child or young adult—whenever you were initially hurting. Or it can be a thoughtful, heartfelt response to the letter you've just written to the deceased.

Writing a letter from the point of view of the other person can result in great comfort and healing because it will enable you to better understand his or her perspective on the situation. Perhaps you can work out some of the reasons things happened (or didn't happen) that have been an ongoing source of pain for you. At any rate, it's almost certain that this greater understanding will result in a stronger bond between you.

How to communicate your letter. This will be quite a personal experience for you, so find a peaceful, secluded place—either in your home, perhaps with lighted candles to lend a sense of ceremony, or in a natural setting at sunrise or sunset to promote quiet reflection. If you can, have a photo of the deceased person in front of you so you'll feel you're actually communicating; then read your letter(s) aloud.

What to do with the letter(s) after reading. If your letter is a positive one intended to be read by others, then present it to the entire family of the deceased or to an individual family member. Make this presentation in person if you can; otherwise, mail the letter with an explanatory note.

On the other hand, if your letter is intended for your eyes only, plan carefully—before the reading—what you wish to do afterward. Here are but a few ideas, each to be carried out with as much respect and ceremony as you can:

- ◆ Roll the letter like a scroll and tie it tightly with ribbon or string secured to a heavy rock, and then toss the rock into the middle of a pond or lake.

- ◆ Taking care not to break litter laws, hand-shred and toss the letter into a strong wind, perhaps from a hilltop or mountaintop.

- ◆ Burn the letter in a fireplace, in a fire pit at the beach or in the mountains, or with a candle in a fire-safe location.

- ◆ Bury the letter in a natural setting or in a hidden location on your own property where it's unlikely to be detected or dug up.

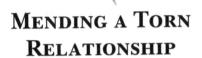

Mending a Torn Relationship

It takes one person to forgive;
it takes two people to be reunited.
—Lewis B. Smedes

Good relationships require care and nurturing. Even then, relationships that have always been good can be unexpectedly upset by an argument or other incident. The problem may result from jealousy, a misunderstanding, an insult directed at you or a family member, a rumor, or a buildup of small resentments that eventually become too much to accept.

Sometimes these upsets blow over quickly and things return to normal. Other times, the situation lasts for days, months, years, or indefinitely. One or both parties may feel unable or unwilling to apologize, ask for forgiveness, offer forgiveness, or otherwise extend an olive branch to the other. So much time can pass that sometimes the parties even forget why they became upset with each other in the first place.

Good Reasons to Reconcile

Meanwhile, borne of a lack of good communication and understanding, the discord eats away at the peace of mind of the individuals involved. Ann Landers (Esther Lederer) offered an interesting perspective on this in her advice column: "Hanging onto resentment is letting someone you despise live rent-free in your head."

Not only is the mind upset by anger and resentment; so is the body. Negative emotions can release adrenaline and cortisol, chemicals that are useful in short-term fight-or-flight responses but are destructive to the immune system when circulated in the bloodstream for extended periods. This could be one of the meanings behind a quotation by Augustine of Hippo (354–430 A.D.), also known as St. Augustine: "Resentment is like taking poison and hoping the other person dies."

Further damage can be wrought on the body. Many believe that the mind does its best to bring into your reality whatever you speak, think, or otherwise focus on. If that's true, then think of the bodily symptoms that may result when someone expresses thoughts such as these:

"He's a real pain in the neck/butt."

"Oh, my aching back; are you serious?"

"I was so upset I could hardly breathe."

"She makes me sick."

"I'm so sick and tired of that guy."

Friends and relatives surrounding this torn relationship can be affected, too. If a friendship breaks up, for example, then people giving a party may rightly invite both their friends who aren't getting along, rather than choose sides. But then one or both of the invitees may place the hosts in an uncomfortable position by asking individually whether the other is planning to attend, and then saying, "Well, I'm not going to be there if he's there, too!" Or, if they both attend, they may either overtly avoid each other or else have a confrontation and thus make other guests uncomfortable.

And what about innocent bystanders within the family— parents, children, siblings, and grandparents? Some family members feel they're forced to choose sides if two of their children or siblings aren't speaking to each other. And how do you manage family holidays together? When there's a schism in the family, peace is destroyed.

With all these unpleasant side effects to anger and upset, you have ample incentive to strive to mend the torn relationship and return to peace and harmony—between the two of you and among those dear to both of you. And that's what the remainder of this chapter is about.

HOW TO STRUCTURE YOUR RECONCILIATION LETTER

Deliver your truth with kindness and compassion. Start with a sincere compliment or other kind statements. Then create an emotional connection between you by mentioning what you've always enjoyed about each other or what you once enjoyed doing together—times you both treasured.

Acknowledge that no two people ever perceive or recall a situation in exactly the same way. As you recall it, truthfully but kindly describe the situation you believe has caused the current upset. Accept responsibility and apologize for any part you may have played in the upset. Then ask for and/or extend forgiveness—whatever is appropriate to the situation.

End with an expression of hope for reconciliation, or at least an agreement to "live and let live," for the sake of personal peace as well as harmony among family and friends who've been affected.

PITFALLS TO AVOID IN YOUR LETTER

In describing what upset you or the other person, avoid starting sentences with "You," such as "You said," and so on. These statements come across as accusations (finger point-ing), automatically putting the other party on the defensive. Instead, describe your own feelings in response to circum-stances at the heart of the upset, e.g.: "I felt bad when I discovered the money was missing from the cookie jar" or "I was devastated when I heard that statement in front of everyone at the party."

Don't discuss other things that have upset you regarding this individual unless they're relevant and will help initiate the dialogue you're hoping for.

RECONCILIATION GOALS FOR SPECIFIC SITUATIONS AND RELATIONSHIPS

In addition to the general advice offered earlier in this chapter, think about the best-case outcomes you're striving for in your unique situation, and keep those goals clearly in mind as you write.

If you're involved in a temporary lovers' quarrel, try to heal the relationship quickly before recollections become distorted and barriers to peace become exaggerated.

If your marriage or partnership is undergoing a long-term separation and you desire reconciliation, try to be sensitive to what the other person is going through as you write. Make a special point to communicate empathy in your letter, even as you explain your hopes for the relationship if or when you reconcile. Suggest compromises that you both might be willing to make.

If you're undergoing a divorce, annulment, or other type of breakup with no intention to reconcile, you can still strive for a "live and let live" relationship between you. Strive for an agreement to be pleasant around each other when attending the same social or family functions. Aim toward being mutually civil and reasonable in your communications about such things such as child custody, family visitation rights, or other potentially volatile circumstances related to your situation. And when your children are involved, propose agreeing to disagree in private; that way your children won't feel caught in the middle or feel compelled to choose sides. They won't be afraid for their own future security and well-being, and they will continue to feel loved.

If you and your parent have had a serious disagreement, reconciliation would certainly be your goal. Try to see the situation from your parent's perspective, and acknowledge any aspect in which you feel your parent was right to act as he or she did. As you explain your own position, do so with kindness and respect. Remember, it isn't a black-and-white, I'm-right-you're-wrong world; shades of gray abound. And if the disagreement had its origins in a conflict between your spouse and your parent, be compassionate; yet remember (and perhaps even remind the participants) that the day you wed, you chose first allegiance to your spouse.

If you and your adult son or daughter had a serious disagreement, step back from the situation to analyze the family dynamics. Was the disagreement related to your son or daughter's need to choose between spouse and parent—to proclaim one of you right and the other wrong? Recall and acknowledge with compassion that on your son or daughter's wedding day, the couple vowed first allegiance to each other, and provide the emotional space for him or her to maintain that allegiance.

Or was the disagreement related to your adult child's perceived need to exercise independence? It can be difficult to let go of control at these times. After all, you've made so many decisions for your child in the past, based on what you felt was best for his or her well being. Now, although you might express an opinion supported by good reasons, you'll need to follow it up by acknowledging that the final decision rests with your adult child.

If your disagreement is with a brother or sister, step back and analyze the family dynamics here. What roles have you each historically played in the family—big brother/sister, middle-child people pleaser, baby of the family? Have you always had sibling rivalries for parental attention or the attention of others? Perhaps some siblings are high achievers, whereas others are more easygoing, preferring to skate through life. Do some siblings feel that their way is the only right way? Do other siblings feel that family members never take them seriously? These roles can be hard to break away from, so compassion and understanding are vital in trying to resolve conflicts between you.

If your disagreement is with a friend, first decide if you want to salvage this friendship. In his book *If I Only Knew Then What I Know Now: The Lessons of Life and What They're Trying to Teach You* (The Creative Syndicate, 2012), Robert Wolff wrote, "Many people don't understand that some friends are only transitory at best. They are in our lives for a short time, then gone" (p. 17). The poem "Reason, Season, or Lifetime" (author unknown) describes the duration and purpose of three types of friendships—those who are in your life for a reason, a season, or a lifetime. You've probably experienced all three, and it's good to recognize which one you're having a problem with now, and why. It could be that it's simply time for each of you to go your respective ways. Even so, it's good to go in peace and goodwill, and that can be the point of your letter, rather than trying to renew the friendship.

However, if your friendship is one whose season has not yet ended or one that you value for its lifetime quality, then do try to reconcile—to renew the friendship for both your sakes. In your letter, work to establish a bond based on the past. Say what you've always appreciated about him or her, and then emphasize that you value the friendship too highly to want to see that bond broken.

How to Present Your Reconciliation Letter

Delivering your letter personally usually isn't the best idea. Why? First, it's unlikely you'd have a good opportunity to do so. Second, even if you did, the individual may refuse to accept it. Third, if the individual did accept it, he or she might feel compelled to read it while you wait. However, you don't want to begin a dialogue until the person has had a chance to privately mull over what you've written. That way, he or she has the opportunity to give a considered response, not an emotionally charged one.

Nor is it appropriate to ask a family member or mutual friend to deliver the letter on your behalf. First, out of a sense of pride, your recipient may be unwilling to accept or read the letter. Second, even if the person did accept the letter, the other family member or friend might remain present while it's being read—and might ask to know the contents. But the contents are highly personal and intended to be private; it's inappropriate for a third party to become involved or influence your recipient's reaction to the letter.

For these reasons, it's best to mail your letter. When you do, it may be better *not* to request a signed proof of delivery, as your recipient may interpret this as a pressure tactic or power play. Instead, you may choose to write "Personal & Confidential—Please Deliver Unopened" just to the right of the return address block to help ensure the privacy you're hoping for.

If you receive no response to your letter within a month, send a brief note. State that you hope the note finds him or her well, you care about your relationship, and you're hoping to hear from him or her regarding the letter you sent on (date). You may want to attach a duplicate copy of the letter, just in case.

With that, you know you've made your best peacemaking effort, so accept the outcome. Next, if you haven't already, forgive yourself for anything you might have done that contributed initially to the upset, because this, too, is healing. Finally, should you find yourself face to face with the other person, behave as if the upset never happened in the first place. This will make it easy, if he or she so desires, to gracefully resume that good relationship, without becoming embarrassed or feeling a need to explain anything.

And if, in the future, any resentment toward him or her creeps back into your thoughts, immediately forgive him or her mentally, and then once again forgive yourself. Repeat as often as needed.

APPENDIX

A. HEARTFELT WORDS TO
   DESCRIBE SOMEONE SPECIAL

B. INSPIRATIONAL THOUGHTS
   TO QUOTE IN YOUR LETTERS

C. GREAT BEGINNINGS TO
   JUMPSTART YOUR SENTENCES

D. MONTHS, WEEKS, AND DAYS
   TO COMMEMORATE
   WITH A LETTER

E. ADDITIONAL RESOURCES

APPENDIX A
HEARTFELT WORDS TO DESCRIBE SOMEONE SPECIAL

A1. A SMALLER CHILD

A2. A PRE-TEEN CHILD

A3. A TEEN BOY

A4. A TEEN GIRL

A5. A YOUNGER MAN

A6. A YOUNGER WOMAN

A7. A MIDDLE-AGED MAN

A8. A MIDDLE-AGED WOMAN

A9. AN OLDER MAN

A10. AN OLDER WOMAN

A11. SOMEONE RELIGIOUS OR SPIRITUAL

A12. A MILITARY SERVICE MEMBER

A13. A SUPERVISOR OR EMPLOYEE

A14. A TEACHER, COACH, MENTOR, OR STUDENT

A15. A PRODUCT CREATOR OR STELLAR SERVICE PROVIDER

A1.
A SMALLER CHILD

Adaptable	Expressive	Peaceful
Adorable	Exuberant	Persistent
Adventurous	Focused	Polite
Affectionate	Fresh	Positive
Ambitious	Friendly	Precious
Brave	Fun	Pretty
Bright	Fun loving	Proud
Calm	Funny	Quick
Carefree	Giving	Quiet
Careful	Good	Serious
Caring	Happy	Shy
Cheerful	Helpful	Smart
Clever	Honest	Strong
Comical	Impetuous	Stubborn
Confident	Independent	Sunny
Cooperative	Kind	Sweet
Creative	Likable	Talented
Curious	Loving	Tidy
Delightful	Magic	Tough
Direct	Mighty	Trusting
Easy going	Mischievous	Truthful
Endearing	Nice	Warm
Energetic	Open	Wise
Engaging	Patient	Witty

A2.
A Pre-Teen Child

Able	Curious	Mature
Accomplished	Delightful	Mechanical
Adaptable	Determined	Mediating
Adept	Do it yourself	Memorable
Admirable	Endearing	Mischievous
Adventurous	Enthusiastic	Nature loving
Artistic	Even tempered	Nonjudgmental
Aspiring	Faithful	Open
Astute	Focused	Outstanding
Athletic	Forgiving	Patient
Authentic	Friendly	Persevering
Aware	Fun loving	Pleasant
Bright	Generous	Problem solving
Brotherly	Gentlemanly	Protective
Calm	Gracious	Quiet
Carefree	Helpful	Reasonable
Charming	Honest	Responsible
Cheerful	Independent	Sensible
Comical	Insightful	Sisterly
Confident	Kind hearted	Sportsmanlike
Considerate	Ladylike	Tactful
Cooperative	Lovable	Understanding
Courageous	Loving	Well rounded
Creative	Loyal	Wholesome

A3.
A TEEN BOY

Adaptable	Handy	Proficient
Adventurous	Helpful	Protective
Ambitious	Honest	Public-spirited
Analytical	Idealistic	Quirky
Artistic	Imaginative	Reasonable
Athletic	Inquisitive	Refreshing
Authentic	Inspiring	Reliable
Bright	Intelligent	Resourceful
Brotherly	Lighthearted	Respectful
Cheerful	Likable	Romantic
Collaborative	Lovable	Self-confident
Conscientious	Loyal	Self-disciplined
Considerate	Mature	Soft hearted
Cooperative	Mischievous	Spontaneous
Courteous	Modest	Sportsmanlike
Energetic	Musical	Studious
Enthusiastic	Nature loving	Supportive
Ethical	Organized	Tactful
Fair minded	Patient	Thoughtful
Fearless	Perceptive	Understanding
Forgiving	Persuasive	Upbeat
Fun loving	Philosophical	Well rounded
Generous	Poetic	Wholesome
Good-natured	Principled	Witty

A4.
A TEEN GIRL

Accomplished	Engaging	Nature loving
Adaptable	Enthusiastic	Nonjudgmental
Adventurous	Ethical	Organized
Affectionate	Fair minded	Outgoing
Ambitious	Focused	Patient
Artistic	Forgiving	Poetic
Athletic	Fun loving	Positive
Authentic	Generous	Public-spirited
Bright	Good-natured	Quiet
Candid	Gracious	Reasonable
Capable	Helpful	Responsible
Caring	Honest	Sensitive
Cheerful	Humane	Sincere
Collaborative	Idealistic	Sisterly
Compassionate	Inquisitive	Spontaneous
Confident	Insightful	Studious
Conscientious	Intelligent	Supportive
Cooperative	Ladylike	Tactful
Courteous	Level headed	Talented
Creative	Likeable	Trustworthy
Devoted	Loyal	Understanding
Disciplined	Modest	Well rounded
Efficient	Moral	Wholesome
Empowered	Musical	Witty

A5.
A YOUNGER MAN

Accomplished	Focused	Persuasive
Adaptable	Forgiving	Philosophical
Adventurous	Fun loving	Poetic
Affectionate	Generous	Practical
Analytical	Gentlemanly	Principled
Artistic	Genuine	Protective
Athletic	Handy	Public-spirited
Brotherly	Helpful	Quirky
Capable	Honest	Reasonable
Clever	Idealistic	Reliable
Comical	Imaginative	Resourceful
Conscientious	Insightful	Romantic
Considerate	Intelligent	Self-confident
Cooperative	Likable	Self-disciplined
Courageous	Lovable	Sensitive
Creative	Loyal	Sincere
Curious	Mature	Spontaneous
Dedicated	Modest	Sportsmanlike
Diplomatic	Musical	Supportive
Direct	Old-fashioned	Talented
Efficient	Open minded	Trustworthy
Engaging	Optimistic	Understanding
Ethical	Passionate	Versatile
Even tempered	Patient	Well read

A6.
A YOUNGER WOMAN

Accomplished

Adventurous

Affectionate

Artistic

Athletic

Bright

Capable

Cheerful

Clever

Compassionate

Considerate

Cooperative

Creative

Dedicated

Diplomatic

Down to earth

Empowered

Engaging

Enthusiastic

Ethical

Forgiving

Fun loving

Generous

Genuine

Gracious

Hard working

Helpful

Honest

Idealistic

Independent

Insightful

Joyful

Kind hearted

Ladylike

Likable

Mischievous

Modest

Musical

Nurturing

Open minded

Organized

Patient

Perceptive

Persuasive

Philosophical

Pleasant

Positive

Practical

Principled

Protective

Resilient

Resourceful

Responsible

Romantic

Self-confident

Selfless

Serene

Service oriented

Sisterly

Spiritual

Spontaneous

Talented

Thoughtful

Tireless

Trustworthy

Unconventional

Unruffled

Versatile

Virtuous

Well liked

Wise

Witty

A7.
A MIDDLE-AGED MAN

Accomplished	Faithful	Paternalistic
Action oriented	Focused	Patient
Adept	Forgiving	Patriotic
Admirable	Fun loving	Persevering
Adventurous	Generous	Persuasive
Affectionate	Gentlemanly	Philosophical
Artistic	Genuine	Playful
Athletic	Good-natured	Poetic
Attentive	Guiding	Principled
Brotherly	Handy	Problem solving
Capable	Helpful	Protective
Caring	Honest	Quiet
Charitable	Indulgent	Rational
Charming	Insightful	Relaxed
Comforting	Inspiring	Self-confident
Considerate	Kind	Smart
Creative	Knowledgeable	Spiritual
Curious	Loyal	Sportsmanlike
Dedicated	Meticulous	Supportive
Efficient	Modest	Thoughtful
Enthusiastic	Motivational	Trustworthy
Ethical	Neighborly	Understanding
Even tempered	Old-fashioned	Versatile
Fair minded	Optimistic	Wise

A8.
A MIDDLE-AGED WOMAN

Accommodating	Fun loving	Philosophical
Adaptable	Generous	Poetic
Affectionate	Gracious	Positive
Ambitious	Hard working	Principled
Artistic	Helpful	Proficient
Caring	Honest	Protective
Charitable	Idealistic	Reliable
Comforting	Inspiring	Religious
Compassionate	Interested	Resourceful
Conscientious	Intuitive	Romantic
Considerate	Joyful	Self-confident
Cooperative	Ladylike	Sensible
Counseling	Likable	Sincere
Courageous	Lovable	Sisterly
Creative	Loyal	Sociable
Dedicated	Meticulous	Soft spoken
Doting	Modest	Spiritual
Down to earth	Musical	Spontaneous
Empowered	Nurturing	Supportive
Enchanting	Open minded	Tactful
Encouraging	Organized	Understanding
Enthusiastic	Patient	Unflappable
Ethical	Perceptive	Versatile
Forgiving	Persuasive	Wise

A9.
AN OLDER MAN

Accomplished	Hospitable	Poetic
Ageless	Humane	Principled
Artistic	Indulgent	Proficient
Authentic	Insightful	Protective
Beloved	Inspiring	Public-spirited
Capable	Intelligent	Purposeful
Caring	Irreplaceable	Reasonable
Cheerful	Jolly	Reliable
Comforting	Kind hearted	Resilient
Creative	Legendary	Resourceful
Curious	Level headed	Salty
Devoted	Lighthearted	Self-educated
Down to earth	Loving	Serious
Eloquent	Loyal	Sportsmanlike
Energetic	Mischievous	Supportive
Engaging	Modest	Thoughtful
Entertaining	Moral	Truthful
Forgiving	Musical	Understanding
Fun loving	Nature loving	Unforgettable
Generous	Neighborly	Upstanding
Gentlemanly	Optimistic	Well liked
Good-natured	Patient	Well read
Helpful	Patriarchal	Wise
Honest	Patriotic	Witty

A10.
AN OLDER WOMAN

Accomplished

Ageless

Artistic

Beloved

Calm

Capable

Charitable

Cheerful

Compassionate

Creative

Devoted

Down to earth

Eloquent

Energetic

Enthusiastic

Ethical

Fair minded

Forgiving

Forthright

Fun loving

Generous

Gracious

Helpful

Honest

Hospitable

Humane

Imaginative

Indulgent

Insightful

Inspiring

Intelligent

Interested

Intuitive

Ladylike

Legendary

Lighthearted

Maternal

Matriarchal

Mischievous

Modest

Musical

Nature loving

Neighborly

Nonjudgmental

Nurturing

Old-fashioned

Optimistic

Philosophical

Poetic

Pragmatic

Public-spirited

Religious

Resilient

Resourceful

Saucy

Self-confident

Self-educated

Sensitive

Sincere

Soft spoken

Spiritual

Supportive

Tactful

Talented

Thoughtful

True

Trustworthy

Understanding

Well liked

Well read

Wise

Witty

A11.
SOMEONE RELIGIOUS OR SPIRITUAL

Abiding

Accepting

Accessible

Attentive

Blessed

Brotherly

Capable

Communicative

Compassionate

Contemplative

Creative

Dedicated

Devout

Diplomatic

Discreet

Eloquent

Engaging

Enthusiastic

Ethical

Fluent

Godly

Good-natured

Guiding

Helpful

Honorable

Hospitable

Humble

Idealistic

Insightful

Inspiring

Interested

Intuitive

Kind hearted

Likable

Merciful

Moral

Motivational

Obedient

Patient

Peaceful

Peacemaking

Perceptive

Philosophical

Positive

Practical

Prayerful

Principled

Radiant

Religious

Resolute

Resourceful

Responsive

Reverent

Righteous

Self-disciplined

Selfless

Service oriented

Sincere

Sisterly

Spiritual

Steadfast

Supportive

Talented

Tireless

Tolerant

Trustworthy

Understanding

Unifying

Virtuous

Visionary

Well read

Wise

A12.
A MILITARY SERVICE MEMBER

Accomplished	Ethical	Public-spirited
Adaptable	Focused	Ready
Adept	Handy	Reliable
Alert	Hard working	Resourceful
Ambitious	Helpful	Sacrificing
Analytical	Heroic	Self-confident
Attentive	Honest	Service oriented
Authentic	Honorable	Sisterly
Authoritative	Idealistic	Smart
Brotherly	Innovative	Stable
Calm	Insightful	Strategic
Capable	Inspiring	Supportive
Caring	Invaluable	Tactical
Compassionate	Knowledgeable	Talented
Conscientious	Loyal	Tough
Cooperative	Modest	True
Courageous	Motivational	Trustworthy
Courteous	No nonsense	Unifying
Dedicated	Observant	Unwavering
Devoted	Outstanding	Valorous
Disciplined	Patriotic	Versatile
Distinguished	Persevering	Well grounded
Effective	Positive	Well liked
Enthusiastic	Praiseworthy	Worthy

A13.
A SUPERVISOR OR EMPLOYEE

Accessible	Flexible	Positive
Accommodating	Focused	Practical
Acknowledging	Forgiving	Principled
Action oriented	Friendly	Productive
Admirable	Fun loving	Professional
Ambitious	Guiding	Proficient
Analytical	Hard working	Punctual
Attentive	Helpful	Reasonable
Authentic	Honest	Receptive
Authoritative	Inquisitive	Reliable
Candid	Instrumental	Resourceful
Capable	Interdisciplinary	Responsible
Collaborative	Interested	Responsive
Conscientious	Invaluable	Self-confident
Considerate	Inventive	Smart
Cooperative	Knowledgeable	Supportive
Creative	Logical	Systematic
Diplomatic	Loyal	Tireless
Direct	Modest	Top notch
Disciplined	Motivational	Trustworthy
Down to earth	Objective	Unwavering
Efficient	Orderly	Versatile
Enthusiastic	Perceptive	Well informed
Ethical	Persevering	Well liked

A14.
A TEACHER, COACH, MENTOR, OR STUDENT

Accessible	Enthusiastic	Practical
Accommodating	Facilitative	Professional
Accomplished	Fair minded	Proficient
Admirable	Firm	Progressive
Ambitious	Focused	Refreshing
Analytical	Forgiving	Reliable
Aspiring	Guiding	Remarkable
Astute	Hard working	Resourceful
Athletic	Helpful	Respectful
Attentive	Idealistic	Self-confident
Authentic	Imaginative	Self-disciplined
Bright	Independent	Serious
Capable	Inquisitive	Sportsmanlike
Collaborative	Insightful	Studious
Conscientious	Inspiring	Supportive
Cooperative	Kind hearted	Talented
Credible	Knowledgeable	Unconventional
Devoted	Methodical	Unforgettable
Diplomatic	Nurturing	Unparalleled
Down to earth	Organized	Validating
Effective	Patient	Well read
Eloquent	Perceptive	Well rounded
Encouraging	Persuasive	Wise
Engaging	Positive	Witty

A15.
A PRODUCT CREATOR OR STELLAR SERVICE PROVIDER

Accommodating	Helpful	Problem solving
Astute	Honest	Professional
Attentive	Imaginative	Quality
Businesslike	Ingenious	Reasonable
Capable	Insightful	Reassuring
Caring	Intelligent	Refreshing
Clever	Invaluable	Reliable
Conscientious	Inventive	Reputable
Courteous	Knowledgeable	Resourceful
Creative	Likable	Responsible
Dedicated	Logical	Service oriented
Diplomatic	No nonsense	Sincere
Discreet	Notable	Skilled
Efficient	Objective	Supportive
Enthusiastic	Observant	Systematic
Ethical	Old-fashioned	Talented
Exacting	Organized	Tireless
Experienced	Original	Top notch
Extraordinary	Outstanding	Understanding
Flexible	Patient	Unparalleled
Focused	Perceptive	Unruffled
Forthright	Persevering	Versatile
Friendly	Positive	Visionary
Guiding	Practical	Wise

APPENDIX B

INSPIRATIONAL THOUGHTS TO QUOTE IN YOUR LETTERS

B1. AGE

B2. APPRECIATION

B3. CHILDREN, PARENTS, AND GRANDPARENTS

B4. FORGIVENESS

B5. LEGACY

B6. LOVE AND FRIENDSHIP

B7. SPIRITUAL FAITH AND DEVOTION

B8. MILITARY AND PATRIOTISM

B9. LEADERSHIP AND TEAMWORK

B10. TEACHING, LEARNING, AND STRIVING

B1.
AGE

I'm youth, I'm joy, I'm a little bird that has broken out of the egg.
—James Matthew Barrie

Youth is, after all, just a moment, but it is the moment, the spark, that you always carry in your heart.
—Raisa M. Gorbachev

Age considers; youth ventures.
—Rabindranath Tagore

Youth is the gift of nature, but age is a work of art.
—Stanislaw Lec

Middle age is youth without levity, and age without decay.
—Doris Day

You can't help getting older, but you don't have to get old.
—George Burns

Wrinkles should merely indicate where smiles have been.
—Mark Twain

There is a fountain of youth: it is your mind, your talents, the creativity you bring to your life and the lives of people you love. When you learn to tap this source, you will truly have defeated age.
—Sophia Loren

Age is an issue of mind over matter. If you don't mind, it doesn't matter.
—Mark Twain

B2.
APPRECIATION

Gratitude is literally one of the few things that can measurably change people's lives.
—Dr. Robert Emmons, Researcher on Gratitude

Gratitude unlocks the fullness of life. It turns what we have into enough, and more. It turns denial into acceptance, chaos to order, confusion to clarity. It can turn a meal into a feast, a house into a home, a stranger into a friend. Gratitude makes sense of our past, brings peace for today, and creates a vision for tomorrow.
—Melody Beattie

No one is more cherished in this world than someone who lightens the burden of another. Thank you.
—Unknown

Feeling gratitude and not expressing it is like wrapping a present and not giving it.
—William Arthur Ward

I would maintain that thanks are the highest form of thought; and that gratitude is happiness doubled by wonder.
—G. K. Chesterton

If the only prayer you said in your whole life was, "thank you," that would suffice.
—Meister Eckhart

Life is not measured by the number of breaths we take but by the number of moments that take our breath away.
—Hilary Cooper

B3.
CHILDREN, PARENTS, AND GRANDPARENTS

Before you were conceived I wanted you
Before you were born I loved you
Before you were here for an hour I would die for you
This is the miracle of life
—Maureen Hawkins

*Parenthood is a partnership with God... you are working with
the creator of the universe in shaping human character
and determining destiny.*
—Ruth Vaughn

*You are the bows from which your children,
as living arrows, are sent forth.*
—Kahlil Gilbran

*When you put faith, hope, and love together, you can raise
positive kids in a negative world.*
—Zig Ziglar

*While we try to teach our children all about life,
our children teach us what life is all about.*
—Angela Schwindt

*Children are like sponges; they absorb all your strength
and leave you limp...
But give them a squeeze and you get it all back.*
—Ann Van Tassells

*The law of love could be best understood and learned
through little children.*
—Mohandas K. Gandhi

*If a child is to keep alive his inborn sense of wonder he needs the
companionship of at least one adult who can share it,
rediscovering with him the joy, excitement and
mystery of the world we live in.*
—Rachel Carson

*She discovered with great delight that one does not love one's
children just because they are one's children but because of
the friendship formed while raising them.*
—Gabriel Garcia Marquez

*Children's children are a crown to the aged, and parents
are the pride of their children.*
—Proverbs 17:6

Grandparents are a family's greatest treasure, the founders of a
loving legacy, the greatest storytellers, the keepers of traditions
that linger on in cherished memory. Grandparents are the
family's strong foundation. Their very special love sets
them apart. Through happiness and sorrow, through
their special love and caring, grandparents keep
a family close at heart.
—Unknown

Grandchildren are God's way of compensating us
for growing old.
—Mary H. Waldrip

B4.
FORGIVENESS

A heart filled with anger has no room for love.
—Joan Lunden

To err is human, to forgive, divine.
—Alexander Pope

To forgive is to set a prisoner free, and to discover
that you are the prisoner set free.
—Lewis B. Smedes

To forgive is the highest, most beautiful form of love. In return,
you will receive untold peace and happiness.
—Robert Muller

"Forgiveness" requires deliberate action on our part.
We acknowledge a wrong has been committed, but
we also choose to release the offender from any
obligation toward us. In essence, we say,
"I will no longer hold this person's
unfair behavior against him."
—Charles Stanley

Forgiveness does not change the past,
but it does enlarge the future.
—Nelson Mandela

Have patience with all things,
but first of all with yourself.
—St. Thomas of Sales

B5.
LEGACY

We will be known forever by the tracks we leave.
—Dakota proverb

How wonderful that nobody need wait a single moment
before starting to improve the world.
—Anne Frank

The only thing you take with you when you're gone
is what you leave behind.
—John Allston

If I have done any deed worthy of remembrance,
that deed will be my monument. If not,
no monument can preserve my memory.
—Agesilaus II

We are not here merely to make a living, but to enrich the world
with a finer spirit of hope and achievement—and we
impoverish ourselves if we forget the errand.
—Woodrow Wilson

We change the world not by what we say or do, but as a
consequence of what we have become.
—David R. Hawkins

*To laugh often and much; to win the respect of intelligent people
and the affection of children; to earn the appreciation of honest
critics and endure the betrayal of false friends; to appreciate
beauty, to find the best in others; to leave the world a bit
better, whether by a healthy child, a garden patch or a
redeemed social condition; to know even one life has
breathed easier because you have lived.
This is to have succeeded.*
—Ralph Waldo Emerson

B6.
LOVE AND FRIENDSHIP

*I love thee to the depth and breadth and height
my soul can reach.*
—Elizabeth Barrett Browning

*The less we look with our eyes, the more
we will see with our hearts.*
—Unknown

*My bounty is as boundless as the sea, my love as deep; the more
I give to thee, the more I have, for both are infinite.*
—William Shakespeare, *Romeo and Juliet*

*The brain does the thinking, but the heart knows more about love
than the mind can ever comprehend.*
—Unknown

*Ancient lovers believed a kiss would literally unite their souls,
because the spirit was said to be carried in one's breath.*
—Eve Glicksman

*For every day, I miss you. For every hour, I need you. For every
minute, I feel you. For every second, I want you.
Forever, I love you.*
—Unknown

True happiness consists not in the multitude of friends,
but in their worth and choice.
—Samuel Johnston

And in the sweetness of friendship let there be laughter, and
sharing of pleasures. For in the dew of little things
the heart finds its morning—and is refreshed.
—Kahlil Gibran

A friend is a present you give yourself.
—Robert Louis Stevenson

A friend is a person with whom I may be sincere.
Before him I may think aloud.
—Ralph Waldo Emerson

B7.
SPIRITUAL FAITH AND DEVOTION

Faith is the bird that sings when the dawn is still dark.
—Rabindranath Tagore

Faith dispels doubt and hesitation, it liberates you from suffering
and delivers you to the city of peace and happiness.
—Dalai Lama

Faith is taking the first step even when you don't see
the whole staircase.
—Martin Luther King, Jr.

Faith is the daring of the soul to go farther than it can see.
—William Newton Clarke

A little faith will bring your soul to heaven, but a lot of faith
will bring heaven to your soul.
—Martin Luther King, Jr.

Faith is a knowledge within the heart, beyond the reach of proof.
—Kahlil Gibran

Life without God is like an unsharpened pencil—
it has no point.
—Unknown

Be who you are and be that well.
—St. François de Sales

All major religious traditions carry basically the same message,
that is love, compassion and forgiveness... the important thing
is they should be part of our daily lives.
—Dalai Lama

In Thy presence is fullness of joy.
—Psalm 16:11

Wait on the Lord: be of good courage, and he shall strengthen
thine heart: wait, I say, on the Lord.
—Psalm 27:14

Meditation has a transforming power in it. The hearing of
the Word may affect us, but the meditating upon it
doth transform us.
—Thomas Watson

Reflection is the lamp of the heart. If it departs,
the heart will have no light.
—Imam Al-Haddad

B8.
MILITARY AND PATRIOTISM

Let us have faith that right makes might, and in that faith let us
to the end dare to do our duty as we understand it.
—Abraham Lincoln

Let every nation know, whether it wishes us well or ill, that we
shall pay any price, bear any burden, meet any hardship,
support any friend, oppose any foe, to assure
the survival and success of liberty.
—John F. Kennedy

*The difficult we do immediately; the impossible
takes a little longer.*
—U.S. Air Force motto

Where there is unity there is always victory.
—Publilius Syrus

*Never in the field of human conflict was so much owed
by so many to so few.*
—Winston Churchill

*How important it is for us to recognize and celebrate
our heroes and she-roes!*
—Maya Angelou

*We often take for granted the very things
that most deserve our gratitude.*
—Cynthia Ozick

*If I had a single flower for every time I think about you,
I could walk forever in my garden.*
—Attributed to Claudia Ghandi

Homecoming means coming home to what is in your heart.
—Unknown

*Freedom has never been free... I love my children and I love
my wife with all my heart. And I would die, die gladly,
if that would make a better life for them.*
—Medgar Evers

*My fellow Americans, ask not what your country can do for you,
ask what you can do for your country.*
—John F. Kennedy

*Patriotism consists not in waving the flag, but in striving
that our country shall be righteous as well as strong.*
—James Bryce

B9.
LEADERSHIP AND TEAMWORK

Management is doing things right; leadership is doing the right things.
—Peter Drucker

A good objective of leadership is to help those who are doing poorly to do well and to help those who are doing well to do even better.
—Jim Rohn

The supreme quality for leadership is unquestionably integrity. Without it, no real success is possible, no matter whether it is on a section gang, a football field, in an army, or in an office.
—Dwight D. Eisenhower

Leadership is the capacity to translate vision into reality.
—Warren G. Bennis

Individually, we are one drop. Together we are an ocean.
—Ryunosuke Satoro

If everyone is moving forward together, then success takes care of itself.
—Henry Ford

Teamwork divides the task and multiples the success.
—Unknown

A group becomes a team when each member is sure enough of himself and his contribution to praise the skills of others.
—Norman Shidle

There ain't no rules around here. We're trying to accomplish something!
—Thomas A. Edison

B10.

TEACHING, LEARNING, AND STRIVING

The truth is that I am enslaved... in one vast love affair
with 70 children.
—Sylvia Ashton-Warner, on life as a teacher

Man's mind, stretched to a new idea, never goes back
to its original dimensions.
—Oliver Wendell Holmes Jr.

The future belongs to those who believe
in the beauty of their dreams.
—Eleanor Roosevelt

Three simple rules for life:
(1) If you don't go after what you want, you'll never have it.
(2) If you don't ask, the answer is always no.
(3) If you don't step forward, you're always in the same place.
—Unknown

Treat people as if they were what they should be, and you help
them become what they are capable of being.
—Johann Wolfgang von Goethe

Anyone who stops learning is old, whether at twenty or eighty.
Anyone who keeps learning stays young. The greatest
thing in life is to keep your mind young.
—Henry Ford

It's what we learn after we know it all that counts.
—John Wooden

Striving for excellence motivates you;
striving for perfection is demoralizing.
—Harriet Braiker

The most splendid achievement of all is the constant striving to surpass yourself and to be worthy of your own approval.
—Denis Waitley

It's kind of fun to do the impossible.
—Walt Disney

APPENDIX C
GREAT BEGINNINGS TO JUMPSTART YOUR SENTENCES

These few pages contain only a small sample of the types of phrases and sentences you might use in your letter as is or adapted. It isn't possible to represent all types of heartfelt letters that might be written, but these will get you started.

Let these entries inspire you to express yourself in a way that is uniquely yours. Just keep this in mind: If you were receiving this letter, what truthful thoughts would you most appreciate reading?

C1. SHARED PAST EXPERIENCES

C2. SHARED PRESENT EXPERIENCES

C3. THOUGHTFUL REFLECTIONS

C4. LEGACY ACKNOWLEDGMENTS

C5. LONGING FOR ANOTHER

C6. CONGRATULATIONS AND/OR LOOKING TO THE FUTURE

C7. RECOMMENDATION/REFERENCE

C8. GENERAL APPRECIATION

C9. MENDING A TORN RELATIONSHIP

C10. EULOGY OR REMEMBRANCE

C11. CONDOLENCES AND APPRECIATION

C1.
SHARED PAST EXPERIENCES

Remember when we used to...?

One of my favorite moments with you was when....

Remember how, when we were kids, we'd go outside and...?

I always appreciated that, when I _____, you came to my rescue and....

When I was _____ years old, one of the most powerful lessons you taught me was....

When I was small, I always looked up to you because _____. Now that we're both older....

Last year, we had some challenges, but I'm thrilled at the way we overcame them together....

C2.
SHARED PRESENT EXPERIENCES

Know what I like best when it's just the two of us...?

I love going to lunch with you because....

To you, it may seem like just getting together for coffee with a friend, but it means so much more to me because....

I always enjoy our time together _____ (e.g., fishing, attending ball games, camping, playing on the team, etc.) because....

Thank you for calling about _____; hearing your voice makes me smile.

When I want _____, you're always there.

I always call you when....

I love laughing with you about....

C3.
THOUGHTFUL REFLECTIONS

You're growing up so quickly. I remember when....

During your educational journey, you have consistently done your best to....

The other day, I was thinking about you and realizing....

When we first met, I thought you were _____. Then I got to know you and realized that wasn't accurate. You are _____!

One of the most important lessons you taught me was....

When I was just getting started in _____ (e.g., business, my career, graduate school, teaching, etc.), you were instrumental in....

Remembering the _____ (joys/sorrows) we shared when _____ (name a shared event) makes me realize what a valuable, treasured friend you are!

The other day I was _____, and I couldn't help thinking of you....

_____ (Grandpa/Grandma), I always thought of you as my _____ (buddy, good friend, best friend) who....

During the past few _____ (e.g., days, weeks, months, years, etc.), you've been able to enjoy _____. It's been a privilege to be part of _____ (e.g., that experience, your life, etc.).

On _____ (Mother's Day/Father's Day), I can't help but realize all the sacrifices you've made....

Whenever I see a flower in bloom, I think of our growing _____ (friendship/relationship) and how much it means to me because....

C4.
LEGACY ACKNOWLEDGMENTS

Looking back on my life, I see you played a vital role in it as....

Do you realize how many lives you've affected?

When I stop to think about the people who have influenced me the most, I think of....

When I think how far I've come _____ (e.g., physically, emotionally, etc.), I realize how much I owe you for your _____ (training/support) along the way....

You are an inspiration to me. I admire your _____ (e.g., strength, courage, compassion, etc.).

_____ (I/We) appreciate having you as _____ (my/our) _____ (e.g., parents, mom, dad, grandpa, grandma, etc.), especially because of how you....

As we advance in years, we build wonderful memories, and you are one of the memories I treasure most. Here's what you've meant to me in my life: _____ (description of feelings here).

Let me tell you what a difference you've made in my life by saying....

Honored ancestor, the strong, positive values you instilled in your children have been passed along through the generations, and as a result....

_____ (I /We) light this candle for you, _____ (ancestor's name); may its flame represent the high esteem in which we hold your memory and your legacy.

C5.
LONGING FOR ANOTHER

I miss you most when....

Soon we'll be together and we can....

We'll miss you after you've left home, but we'll be as near as your heart....

Even though we'll miss you greatly, you have our full support in your decision....

On your impending retirement, _____ (I /we) hope you know how greatly you'll be missed because of your....

C6.
CONGRATULATIONS AND/OR LOOKING TO THE FUTURE

I'm looking forward to....

_____ (Your/Our) new baby is so lucky because....

We may have challenges as new parents, but we'll also have....

My goodness—your first day of school! I'm so proud of you, and I know you will....

You're about to embark on a grand new educational adventure, and I know you will....

You're about to become a young woman, and I know you will....

We'll miss you when you've moved out, but we know you will....

Your _____ (moving/joining the military) may change the dynamics of our _____ (friendship/relationship), but it will never extinguish it because....

The _____ (medal/award) you've received has been well deserved because....

You're about to be my partner in life, and I couldn't be happier because....

In the coming year, I wish for you _____ and I wish for us together _____.

We're so honored that you're becoming part of the family because....

We're proud to welcome you as our new _____ (son-in-law/daughter-in-law) and wish you....

Now that you've been accepted as a young man in our _____ (e.g., community, temple, synagogue, mosque, ashram, church, ward, tribe, etc.), I know you'll be an asset because....

Your profession of faith honors _____ (e.g., God, Allah, the Buddha, Krishna, Universe, Higher Power, etc.), as well as those here on Earth who love you. _____ (I/We) admire your decision because....

Congratulations on your profession of faith to become _____; you will be a genuine asset to _____ (your/our) religious community as you go forth in service because....

The company is pleased to report an excellent _____ (quarter/year) in which _____ goals were attained. In recognition of the important role you've played in our success, you will be receiving _____ (description of bonus award) on _____ (date). Congratulations and keep up the good work!

Congratulations! We are pleased to inform you that your qualifications have exceeded those of the other applicants for the position of _____ within _____ department at our _____ location. This letter is an offer of employment involving the following details: (e.g., job title, salary, working hours, effective date, etc.). Please indicate your acceptance or rejection of this offer by _____ (description of method or action to be taken) no later than _____ (date).

You've enjoyed _____ years at _____ (company name), and we appreciate your loyalty and hard work.

You've worked hard, and your retirement is so well deserved because....

Your retirement is the beginning of a new, exciting phase in your life.

Congratulations. Your retirement will finally afford you the opportunity to....

C7.
RECOMMENDATION/REFERENCE

I am pleased to recommend _____ (candidate's name) for the position of _____. It has been my honor as _____ (his/her) _____ to observe firsthand _____ (his/her) _____ (description of positive qualities relating to job description or good character).

Over the years as the _____ (supervisor/employer) of _____ (candidate's name), I have especially appreciated _____ (description of positive qualities relating to job description or good character).

In response to your request for a _____ (recommendation/ reference) relating to _____ (candidate's name)'s application for _____ (name of position), I'm pleased to report....

_____ (Name) was my student at _____ (educational institution) for _____ (class name or internship name). I am honored to recommend _____ (him/her) for _____ (e.g., name of scholarship, type of internship, employment, etc.), based on _____ (his/her) exemplary qualities that include _____ (description of those qualities, specifically orienting them to the student's desired goal).

C8.
GENERAL APPRECIATION

You're my favorite....

I really appreciate how you....

I love that....

Now that we've known each other for (e.g., a while, so long, a few months, etc.), let's....

_____ (Name), thank you so much for being in my life...

You may not realize it, but you've given me lots of joy. I love so many things about you, including....

I'm glad we're finally talking about....

You bring so much _____ in to my life. I really appreciate how you _____ because....

Your friendship is important to me. You're always there with words of support or a helping hand when....

It's amazing how quickly you've grown and matured!

I'm so proud of you for improving your grades, but I can't say I'm surprised. After all, you....

You've worked hard to earn your _____ (e.g., professional certification, associate degree, master's degree, doctorate, etc.). This honor is well deserved and will serve you well as you go forward to....

I remember back in _____ (name of grade or class) when you taught us that fantastic _____ (e.g., formula, fact, principle, mnemonic device, etc.). I've used what you taught in so many aspects of my life since then, and have shared it with countless others. Thank you for being my teacher.

When you were in my _____ class, I remember how you influenced the whole learning environment, especially the way you _____ (e.g., added to the discussion, brought up new ways of thinking, etc.).

I always appreciated your comments in class, as well as your support when other students attempted to undermine a positive learning environment. Thank you. I know you'll do well in life because....

Thank you for your recent efforts on the _____ project for _____ (customer's name). You were instrumental in assuring that the customer's needs were met or exceeded _____ (e.g., on time, on budget, etc.). _____ (I/We) especially appreciated that you _____ (e.g., worked long hours, remained on call, traveled to the customer site, etc.). You are a valuable addition to both the department and the company.

I really _____ (enjoy/appreciate) your _____ (description of product or service). What I especially like is....

Your _____ (product/service) came to my rescue when....

_____ (Name), _____ (e.g., you, your product, your company's product, your service, etc.) has made such a difference to me because....

The _____ service you provide me has made a wonderful difference in _____ (e.g., my business success, my clients' projects, my/our lifestyle, my/our house, my/our yard, etc.) because....

The way you and your company solved my recent problem with your _____ (e.g., product, service, warranty, etc.) was remarkably satisfactory because _____ (description of details). As a result of this experience, I have been converted from being an unhappy customer into being a genuine fan who will tell others about the great way you solved my problem. Thank you.

They say word of mouth is always the best form of advertising. The words from your mouth have been a great boost to my business, and I appreciate you greatly because....

I have just begun to work with _____ (name of new client or customer) and am so grateful for your high praise and strong recommendation that made this business relationship possible.

I have just been awarded the biggest contract of my business career, and I owe it to you because of....

Your ongoing business referrals have meant so much to my business and to me.

C9.
MENDING A TORN RELATIONSHIP

I always treasured the times when you and I would _____, and I'd like to see those good times happen again.

Somehow, and for whatever reason, we have been out of touch, and I truly regret it. Can we _____ (e.g., make a fresh start, get together, have a phone conversation, etc.)?

I miss you, and I'd like to see you be part of my life again because....

I hope whatever has come between us can be mended. I miss you greatly and would like to have you in my life once again because....

I think I may know what came between us, and I apologize from the bottom of my heart. Our relationship was so great before; I'd like to have you back in my life because....

C10.
EULOGY OR REMEMBRANCE

_____ (Name) may be gone, but _____ (his/her) influence lives on. I remember when....

When we think of _____ (Name), let's be honest: There may be mixed feelings. But today is a day to remember the good, and there is much to remember....

I always loved it when _____ (Name) would....

Some of you recall the time that we were at the _____ (park, stadium, etc.), _____ (doing/playing) _____, and _____ (Name) made us all _____ (e.g., laugh, wonder, think twice, etc.).

I'll never forget how _____ (Name) would _____ whenever we were together. It always made me _____ (laugh/cry/think).

C11.
CONDOLENCES AND APPRECIATION

Your _____ (e.g., husband, wife, son, daughter, etc.) was a credit to _____ (his/her) country, and we will all miss _____ (him/her) greatly. Please accept _____ (my/our) condolences for your loss.

The sacrifice your _____ (e.g., husband, wife, son, daughter, etc.) made for his/her country hasn't gone unremembered or unappreciated. I recall....

_____ (Name) meant a lot to me in my life. _____ (He/She) would always....

_____ (date) will mark a year since _____ (Name) died, and I wanted to take a moment to let you know I'm thinking of _____ (him/her) and of you. _____ (Name) was a wonderful _____ (brother, sister, friend, cousin, etc.) who always did _____ (description of something meaningful). We miss _____ (him/her) so much. I'll call you in a couple of days to see if you'd like to get together to toast _____ (his/her) memory and talk about the good times we had together....

I'm writing to let you know that _____ (Name) is still in my heart, and I'd like to offer my support. Please let me know....

It's been a year since we lost _____ (Name), and I'm thinking of both of you.

_____ (Name) is never far from my thoughts. The other day, I was thinking, "Gosh, I ought to tell _____ (Name) about this; _____ (he'd/she'd) really get a kick out of it." Then I remembered.

_____ (Name) was a great friend, and I'll always be glad to have known _____ (him/her).

Appendix D

Months, Weeks, and Days to Commemorate with a Letter

January

National Thank You Month

New Year's Day *(January 1)*

Cuddle Up Day *(January 6)*

Peculiar People Day *(January 10)*

National Hugging Day *(January 21)*

Compliment Day *(January 24)*

February

International Friendship Month

Valentine's Day *(February 14)*

Random Acts of Kindness Week *(apparently the second full Monday-through-Sunday week; verify dates each year at RandomActsOfKindness.org)*

Random Acts of Kindness Day *(occurs during Random Acts of Kindness Week; verify date each year at RandomActsOfKindness.org)*

Family Day *(Canada; third Monday)*

March

Share a Smile Day *(March 1)*

First Day of Spring *(March 20 in U.S.)*

APRIL

National Poetry Month

Administrative Professionals Day *(fourth Wednesday)*

Hug a Friend Day *(April 26)*

MAY

Older Americans Month

Teacher Appreciation Week *(first full Monday-through-Friday week)*

National Teachers' Day *(always Tuesday of Teacher Appreciation Week)*

Mother's Day *(second Sunday)*

Visit Your Relatives Day *(May 18)*

Armed Forces Day *(U.S.; third Saturday)*

Memorial Day *(last Monday)*

JUNE

Ball Point Pen Day *(June 10)*

Flag Day *(June 14)*

Power of a Smile Day *(June 15)*

Father's Day *(third Sunday in U.S.)*

JULY

National Picnic Month

Cheer Up the Lonely Day *(July 11)*

AUGUST

Respect for Parents Day *(August 1)*

Friendship Day *(first Sunday)*

National Smile *Week (second Sunday-through-Saturday week)*

Be an Angel Day *(August 22)*

Kiss and Make Up Day *(August 25)*

SEPTEMBER

Women of Achievement Month

Grandparents Day *(first Sunday after Labor Day)*

Patriot Day, also known as World Trade Center
Remembrance Day *(U.S.; September 11)*

National Stepfamily Day *(September 16)*

World Gratitude Day *(September 21)*

Good Neighbor Day *(September 28)*

OCTOBER

Family History Month

World Teachers' Day *(October 5)*

Thanksgiving Day *(Canada; second Monday)*

Sweetest Day *(third Saturday; a day to make someone happy)*

National Boss Day *(October 16, if a weekday; otherwise, the
working day nearest to October 16)*

NOVEMBER

El Día de los Muertos, also known as The Day of the Dead
*(Latin American countries; November 1. In Mexico,
celebrated an entire week)*

Veterans Day *(U.S.; November 11)*

Remembrance Day *(Canada; November 11)*

Universal Children's Day *(November 20)*

Thanksgiving *(U.S.; fourth Thursday in November)*

DECEMBER

Write to a Friend Month

New Year's Eve *(December 31)*

APPENDIX E
ADDITIONAL RESOURCES

Because Web-based information can change frequently, Appendix E consists primarily of key-word suggestions for conducting your own Web search regarding areas that interest you. You will also find selected websites listed on the Resources page of GoodWaysToWrite.com.

STATIONERY AND PENS

Search the Web using these key words:

- fine stationery
- specialty papers
- fine writing instruments
- fountain pens

Also visit the Resources page of GoodWaysToWrite.com

FRAMES, FRAME STANDS, FOLDERS, BINDERS, BINDING, AND ELEGANT GIFT-WRAPPING AND SCRAPBOOKING PAPER

Search the Web using these key words:

- picture frames
- document frames
- sign holders
- frame stands
- display stands
- folders
- binders
- bindery services
- elegant gift wrapping paper

Also visit the Resources page of GoodWaysToWrite.com

SCRAPBOOKING SOFTWARE, PAPER, AND SUPPLIES

Search the Web using these key words:
- scrapbooking software
- scrapbooking supplies
- scrapbooking papers

Also visit the Resources page of GoodWaysToWrite.com

SONG TITLES, LYRICS, MOTION PICTURES, POETRY, AND GRAPHIC IMAGES

Visit the Resources page of GoodWaysToWrite.com

GRAPHIC AND FINE ARTISTS, PHOTOGRAPHERS, POETS, MUSICAL COMPOSERS, RECORDING ARTISTS, AND PERFORMERS

Visit the Resources page of GoodWaysToWrite.com

DICTIONARY, THESAURUS, SPELLER, AND OTHER WRITING TIPS

Visit the Writing Tips page of AllMyBest.com

Also visit the Resources page of GoodWaysToWrite.com

COPYEDITING SUPPORT

Visit AllMyBest.com to learn more about copyediting services offered by the author.

AUDIOVISUAL TOOLS

Search the Web using these key words:
- voice recognition software
- free conference calling
- free video calling
- free audio editing software
- audio recording services
- audio recording software

Also visit the Resources page of GoodWaysToWrite.com

BOOKS AND WORKBOOKS

Visit The Resources page of GoodWaysToWrite.com for a list of quality books related to gratitude and legacy.

MORE WAYS TO SHARE LOVE, APPRECIATION, AND LEGACY

Visit the Resources page of GoodWaysToWrite.com for the latest updates on worthwhile advice sources, organizations, and causes personally endorsed by the author.

Visit the Products pages of GoodWaysToWrite.com for a growing list of Appreciation-based tools to make this world a better place for all of us.

Afterword

It's never too late to learn these values and reflect them in the spirit of the letters you write:

Honor

Appreciation

Generosity

Forgiveness

Consideration

Respect

Spontaneity

Kindness

Loyalty

Trustworthiness

Sportsmanship

Tact

Love for One Another

May others learn from you and spread these heartfelt values far and wide. And through this process, may we heal our relationships and our world.

Acknowledgments

This is my own heartfelt letter of appreciation to those who were instrumental in birthing this book:

To Byron and Rachael Smith, my son and daughter-in-law who, when they married, each wrote and presented framed letters of appreciation to their respective parents (which made me realize how wonderful it would be if more letters of appreciation were written worldwide);

To the voice in my head (and the Higher Power it represents) that, when I wondered aloud in late 2011 whether to write this book, gently but distinctly answered, "Your book will be published by August 15";

To my husband, Ben Smith, whose quiet ongoing support on all fronts gave me the time, space, and freedom to write;

To my human sources of inspiration, Karen Aker, Sharon Lund, David Milligan, Pearl White, and Robert Wolff, for showing me fresh perspectives and believing in me;

To Flora Brown, Andrea Glass, Suanne Lusk, and Pearl White, who suggested valuable additions and refinements to the book's contents;

To my editor, Barbara McNichol of Barbara McNichol Editorial, and my cover designer, Victoria Vinton of Coyote Press, for sharing their exceptional talents;

To the many helpful individuals who generously shared their expertise in the following subject areas—

TEACHERS AND STUDENTS
Flora Brown (Retired Professor, Fullerton
College, Fullerton, California) and Linda Carta
(Retired Teacher, Frank M. Wright Elementary
School, El Monte, California);

MILITARY
Sgt. Gilbert Serrano (Orange, California, Army
Recruiting Office), my father-in-law Ben H. Smith
Sr. (Army Veteran, World War II), and my
husband Ben H. Smith Jr. (Army Veteran,
Vietnam War);

EMPLOYMENT
Helen Parker (Human Resources Consultant,
ParkerHR, Huntington Beach, California);

HOSPICE
Jon Radulovic (Vice President Communications,
National Hospice & Palliative Care Organization);

EULOGIES
Suzanne Stover (Funeral Counselor, McAulay
& Wallace Mortuary, Fullerton, California) and
Tasha Van Horn (Professor, Communications,
Citrus College, Glendora, California);

To my friend and mentor, Eleanore Rankin, for having
encouraged me for decades to write a book and who has
finally seen it happen;

And finally, to God, for manifesting the time and resources
needed to write and publish this book, for keeping me
peaceful in the process, and for giving me the words when I
needed them, so I could share them with the world.

My deepest gratitude to you all.

LYNETTE M. SMITH

ABOUT THE AUTHOR

Since 2004, Lynette M. Smith has headed the business and nonfiction copyediting division of All My Best (AllMyBest.com). In 2009, she expanded her company in order to publish helpful writing guides, now also including her comprehensive reference book *How to Write Heartfelt Letters to Treasure: For Special Occasions and Occasions Made Special*. She holds memberships in Editorial Freelancers Association, San Diego Professional Editors Network, and Publishers & Writers of San Diego.

Both personally and professionally, Lynette abides by the principles in *The Four Agreements* by don Miguel Ruiz: *Be impeccable with your word; don't take anything personally; don't make assumptions; and always do your best.*

A personal event inspired Lynette to write about how to compose and send treasured letters of appreciation. As she tells this story:

> When our son Byron married Rachael in 2008,
> they each wrote a loving letter to their own parents,
> describing not only their fondest childhood memories
> but also the values, life lessons, and ideals they would
> bring to their marriage. At the wedding rehearsal, one
> at a time, they presented their letters to their parents.
> Both sets of parents, as well as all others present,
> felt deeply moved. We will always treasure our
> loving memento.

Inspired by Byron and Rachael's heartfelt creativity, Lynette published a set of four marriage-themed tips booklets for the various types of letters of appreciation.

The book you now hold is Lynette's latest project related to her *big, achievable goal:* to get millions of people worldwide to focus on love and gratitude. One way to accomplish this is for people to start writing heartfelt letters of appreciation to their friends, loved ones, and business associates; these letters can help establish, grow, enhance, or even rebuild personal and professional relationships.

Also in line with her *big, achievable goal,* Lynette is developing a number of additional appreciation-themed projects that can be used and enjoyed in educational, personal, and professional settings.

Lynette hopes you will visit GoodWaysToWrite.com soon to learn more about how

> *"Together we can change the world,
> one heartfelt letter at a time."*

Lightning Source UK Ltd.
Milton Keynes UK
UKOW06f0259280616

277222UK00013B/187/P